Moments of Reflection

Moments of Reflection

L. D. Johnson

Maryneal Jones, Editor

Broadman Press
Nashville, Tennessee

Gateway Seminary Library

© Copyright 1980 • Broadman Press
All rights reserved.
4252-87
ISBN: 0-8054-5287-7

Unless otherwise marked, Scripture quotations are the author's translations.

Scripture quotations marked KJV are from the King James Version of the Bible.

Scripture quotations marked TEV are from the *Good News Bible,* the Bible in Today's English Version. Old Testament: Copyright © American Bible Society 1976; New Testament: Copyright © American Bible Society 1966, 1971, 1976. Used by permission.

Scripture quotations marked RSV are from the Revised Standard Version of the Bible, copyrighted 1946, 1952, © 1971, 1973.

Scripture quotations marked Phillips are reprinted with permission of Macmillan Publishing Co., Inc. from J. B. Phillips: *The New Testament* in Modern English, Revised Edition. © J. B. Phillips 1958, 1960, 1972.

Scripture quotations marked NEB are from *The New English Bible.* Copyright © The Delegates of the Oxford University Press and the Syndics of the Cambridge University Press, 1961, 1970. Reprinted by permission.

Scripture quotations marked Moffat are from *The Bible: a New Translation* by James A. R. Moffat. Copyright © 1935 by Harper and Row, Publishers, Inc. Used by permission.

Scripture quotations marked Williams are from *The New Testament, a Translation in the Language of the People,* by Charles B. Williams. Copyright 1937 and 1966. Moody Press, *Moody Bible Institute of Chicago.* Used by permission.

Dewey Decimal Classification: 242

Subject heading: MEDITATIONS

Library of Congress Catalog Card Number: 80-67779

Printed in the United States of America

Gateway Seminary Library

DEDICATION

To my grandchildren

Carole and Laura Yeatts

and

David and Mark Johnson

"Suffer little children, and forbid them not, to come unto me: for of such is the kingdom of heaven" (Matt. 19:14).

Acknowledgments

The quotation from John Hick on page 14 is from *Evil and the God of Love,* rev. ed. (New York: Harper & Row, 1978), p. 281.

The James Weldon Johnson poetry quotations, pages 21 and 23, are from *God's Trombones* (New York: Viking Press, 1927), p. 40.

The quotation from Eric Hoffer on page 31 is from *The True Believer* (New York: Harper & Row, 1951), p. 120.

The NASA director is quoted on page 37 from "Leadership, The Campus and Integrity," *Faculty Development Newsletter* (Hays, Kansas: Fort Hays Kansas State College, 1975).

Huston Smith is the American scholar quoted on page 38. He is quoted from Earl McGrath, "Careers, Values and General Education," *Liberal Education* (Lilly Foundation, 1974), p. 293.

Martin Gross is quoted on page 48 from *The Psychological Society* (New York: Random House, 1978), p. 3.

Karl Menninger is quoted on page 50 from *Whatever Became of Sin?* (New York: Hawthorn Books, 1973), p. 48.

Oscar Wilde is quoted on page 59 from *Ballad of Reading Gaol* (New York: E. P. Dutton, 1928), III, 37.

Quotations from C. S. Lewis on page 61 are from *Surprised by Joy* (New York: Harcourt, Brace & Co., 1955), p. 237.

Ernest Fremont Tittle is quoted on page 77 from *A Mighty Fortress* (New York: Harper & Brothers, 1949), p. 175.

Albert Schweitzer is quoted on page 77 from *The Edge of the Primeval Forest* (London: Adam and C. Black, 1948), p. 116.

Harry Emerson Fosdick is quoted on pages 79-80 from *The Living of These Days* (London: SCM Press, Ltd., 1957), p. 75.

John Gardner is quoted on page 83 from *Self-Renewal* (New York: Harper & Row, 1964), pp. 14-15.

The hymn quoted on pages 88-89 is "Strong Son of God, Immortal Love," by Alfred Lord Tennyson.

William J. Lederer is quoted on page 103 from *Marriage: For and Against* (New York: Hart Publishing Co., Inc., 1972), p. 136.

Joseph Califano is quoted on page 103 from "Rising Concern Over Surge in Illegitimacy," *U. S. News & World Report,* 16 June 1978, p. 59.

Albert Schweitzer is quoted on page 124 from *Out of My Life and Thought* (New York: Henry Holt & Co., 1933), p. 280.

The work of Dean Kelley's from which Kelley's ideas on pages 124-126 came is *Why Conservative Churches Are Growing* (New York: Harper & Row, 1972).

The anonymous hymn "I Sought the Lord, and Afterward I Knew" is quoted on page 148.

Rolf Hockhuth is quoted on page 156 from *The Deputy* (New York: Grove Press, Inc., 1964), p. 155.

The statement quoted on page 163 is attributed to Henry Ford.

Preface

We were at Seabrook Island off the Charleston, South Carolina coast, my son and I, to finish editing this book. Friends had allowed us to use their villa in a lovely family resort where the North Edisto River meets the Atlantic. Every day, to keep mental and physical processes working, we jogged the island trails.

One day as we loped along a narrow wooden bridge spanning one of the island lagoons, a wild duck in the water below paddled furiously to keep pace with us. Working with L. D. Johnson is like that: paddling furiously to match the social, intellectual, and spiritual challenges he both writes about and lives.

I have known this dear and gentle prophet about eight years, since we crossed paths daily at Furman University where I worked. It was for love that I offered to edit his most recent and deeply personal book, *The Morning After Death*, and for the recognition of a fine word needed in a world that reads too much trash in the name of religion.

After its publication, colleagues and friends began to ask, "When are you going to do a book of his columns?" No one asked whether such a book was planned or suggested that a collection of weekly newspaper columns would be desirable. It was not "whether" but "when." Then L. D.'s wife, Marion, got into the act. "I'll help," she said, as she does with every undertaking involving her family. Then his secretary, Gene Cantrell, began thrusting old copies of his columns at me. I tried to escape by visiting my friend Ann Merline, and as I walked through her back door, she said, "Look, these are the ones I've clipped and saved through the years." The slow process of selecting and editing from twenty years of L. D. Johnson's newspaper columns soon began.

I am happy to commend to you the reading of L. D. Johnson's select columns. Indeed, we paddle furiously, like the mallard, to keep up, but our Mentor waits for us on the trail, understanding us, loving us, forgiving us, blessing us, lifting us when we fall, pointing us always to our loving Father and Redeemer.

MARYNEAL JONES

Contents

I.	Close Encounters with God	11
II.	Do You Believe?	29
III.	A Time to Laugh	46
IV.	Coping	63
V.	No Place to Run	81
VI.	Is Marriage Obsolete?	98
VII.	Turning On or Tuning In	115
VIII.	A Satisfactory Friend	135
IX.	Where Peace Begins	144
X.	Who Says You're Through?	152

I

Close Encounters with God

1

Times of recognition, when something previously unknown becomes known, happen to everyone and provide one of life's best payoffs. These are "Ah, ha!" moments, when we are filled with elation for having claimed for ourselves another small piece of the measureless mystery, converting it to knowledge. "So that's how it works! So that is the name of that tune! So that is who he is!"

See the delight in a child's eyes when suddenly he catches on to a parlor game or discovers how to work a puzzle. He can't wait to try it on some uninitiated soul.

Remember your satisfaction at mastering the manual that came with your child's unassembled Christmas toy? At midnight in the basement suddenly you were Edison and Einstein reincarnated in one mastermind. You should be recruited for the space shuttle program.

The "Ah, ha!" experience happens regularly to creative people. Breakthroughs may come unexpectedly, like a wildcat oil driller striking black gold. Or they may come at the end of a carefully-designed and well-executed plan. The payoff is the excitement of an unexpected gift or else the satisfaction of achieving an anticipated result.

When Albert Schweitzer, a man of prodigious talents, was a small boy he heard people singing music in parts for the first time. Schweitzer, who was to become one of Europe's foremost organists, remembered that the sound of harmony moved him so profoundly he felt faint and had to lean against a wall to keep from falling. "So this is what music sounds like," his mind whispered to itself. "Ah, ha!"

When John Keats was nineteen years old he first read Chapman's "Homer." So profoundly did the Greek poet's words affect him that Keats wrote of that experience:

> Then felt I like some watcher of the skies
> When a new planet swims into his ken;
> Or like stout Cortez, when with eagle eyes
> He stared at the Pacific—and all his men
> Look'd at each other with a wild surmise—
> Silent, upon a peak in Darien.

You may not be a Schweitzer or a Keats, but I shall be very surprised if you know nothing about "Ah, ha!" experiences. They happen to me most often when I am studying the Bible —something I have been doing seriously for more than four decades.

I shall be reading some passage I know like a close friend when all of a sudden something leaps at me that I never saw before. All along it was there, but I had been reading right past it. This time it arrests me, says, "Stop, look, listen." And I sometimes get up and pace back and forth, saying to myself, "You dummy, it was there all the time."

If we are comfortable with the fact that we all have moments of illumination about a problem in our work or play or interpersonal relationships, why should we be uneasy about God breaking in upon our minds and hearts in such an unanticipated way? But the idea of an epiphany, a manifestation of God, a sudden "rending of the skies," makes us uncomfortable. The possibility that God might directly confront us through the Bible or a sermon or a friend or a personal crisis is too unsophisticated for many of us. It's a little spooky.

We much prefer to think of God as a distant relative who sends greetings from some remote distance through a series of messengers, somewhat like the pony express of the old wild West. We expect him to be polite enough to remain incognito.

I don't want anybody telling me how I have to experience God, so I shouldn't try to program your spiritual exercises. But it is clear that the people of the Bible encountered the Divine in moments of sudden recognition.

Moses did at the burning bush. Isaiah was overwhelmed when he saw the Lord in the Temple the year King Uzziah died. Jeremiah heard God calling him to prophesy, and remonstrated that he was unqualified for such a consuming task.

On the day of Christ's resurrection two men walked along a road with him and later recognized who he was when he blessed and broke the bread at supper. Paul fell on the Damascus road at the voice which said, "Saul, Saul, why do you go on persecuting me?" (Acts 9:4). Peter and John and others met him on a lakeshore by dawn's early light.

And it keeps happening. Augustine, Luther, Wesley—the list is too long and the people too honorable to brush the matter off as self-delusion. And what of you? Any close encounters? Any "Ah, ha!" moment when the reality of transcendence broke through and at least for the time arrested you?

If not, make sure you haven't made it impossible by deciding ahead of time that it is impossible. Make sure you are not too preoccupied—maybe with yourself—for even God to get your attention. Make sure you are not choosing to sit in darkness and then complain of the absence of light.

2

The Divine Restraint

Years ago when I was a pastor, on Sunday morning I nearly always would charge my spiritual battery by visiting a children's Sunday School department, collecting messy kisses and hugs. The miracle of childhood was an inspiration, but so was the beauty of adulthood illustrated by the teachers' care for other people's children.

Mature, successful, busy adults were putting themselves on the children's level so that the children might begin to understand God and life. Many of those teachers confirmed my conviction that the best and wisest should teach the most teachable—children. Memories of those Sunday morning visits are among my happy recollections of church.

Thinking about those teachers reminds me of what God has done for us. He has met us at our level. He has given us as much of himself as we can take and still be free to be ourselves.

John Hick, a devout theologian, says that God created man and set him at "epistemic distance" from himself. He did not overwhelm man with the divine "Godness." He did not blind man's spiritual eyes by setting him too close to the divine Sun. He gave man room, distance, freedom to say "No" to his Creator.

Why would God do this? Hick asks. Not to do so would be to make man less than God intended him to be. It would be to make man not free to choose, and thus not really man, but something less than man. Freedom exists only where one has a genuine choice. God bids man to choose to be obedient, but he may not compel obedience, else both God and man lose.

Love cannot exist under compulsion. Faith is not faith unless unfaith is a genuine option. Relationship is rich and mutually fulfilling in direct proportion to its mutual voluntariness.

Therefore, God subtly offers himself to us. He doesn't come on so strong as to overwhelm us. The Bible reports man's experience with God in just this way. It says that man cannot see God face-to-face. We see only God's backside, as my friend Carlyle Marney used to say. Man is Job hearing the Almighty's voice out of the whirlwind. He is Elijah experiencing God "in the sound of a gentle stillness" (1 Kings 19:12). He is Moses encountering God in a burning bush.

When Moses stood on the sacred mountain at Sinai and heard from God that he was to return to Egypt to become his people's deliverer, he asked for God's identification. Before following him, the people would surely demand to know who had sent Moses. "Who shall I say sent me? What is your Name?" God's answer is a mysterious, undefinable word. "My name is I AM. Tell them I AM sent you" (Ex. 3:13-14).

We Christians believe that God materialized himself, enfleshed himself in Jesus Christ, so that we say with confidence, "The Word became flesh" (John 1:14, RSV). Look at Jesus, we say, and you see the likeness of God.

But the "epistemic distance" remains. Were there no possibility of doubt there would be no room for faith. Were there no mystery there would be no worship, and no cause to worship. To worship what I fully understand is idolatry. Those who were with Jesus did not presume to compass him about with their understanding, but gratefully observed and accepted the mystery of him.

God who came in Jesus Christ is not a wrangler or a shouter. He does not override other persons' rights. He does not come on like "gangbusters," knocking down doors, and forcing himself on us.

There is a certain fineness about God's love. He is not reticent about giving us his love, but is careful not to destroy our capacity to say whether or not we want it. He deals with us ever so carefully, as would one who does not wish to break the slender stalk of a bruised reed, as one who does not blow too hard upon a smoking wick lest he extinguish its struggling flame.

This is the divine restraint with which God shows his profound respect and love for us. There are times when we wish he would be bolder, times when he seems to disappear totally, his being swallowed by movements in history or experiences in personal life. The best and most loyal of his people have known such desolation.

But the tentativeness of knowing only his backside is the price we pay for the right freely to believe and to love God.

3

Knowing and Doing God's Will

How can we know God's will? To begin, don't suppose that whatever happens is God's will. Some well-meaning people resign themselves to gruesome events that defy decency with "We must not question the will of God. He makes no mistakes." But God is no supervillain of the universe. Because God made the universe to operate under law lest we all be destroyed by chaos, and because he made us free to hurt ourselves and each other, much happens that God could not intend and still be God.

Neither is God's will automatically whatever you and I want. That is to make ourselves God, providing divine sanction for what is often selfish, even brutish, behavior. People have burned other people at the stake in the name of the will of God. We need a rubric more reliable than "let your conscience be your guide."

Can we know God's will? That depends upon what we mean by the question. I don't think God hands out instruction sheets every morning to the faithful. God is the best of all parents (Jesus said to call him "Father"), and a wise parent does not cripple a child by preventing that child's development into a mature, choice-making adult.

Yes, we know God's will. The prophet Micah put it timelessly: "What does the Lord require of you/but to do justice, and to love kindness,/and to walk humbly with your God?" (Mic. 6:8, RSV). Justice, kindness, humility—those are qualities God wants developed in us.

"But that is so general," someone protests. "Surely you can be more specific. After all, everybody knows that justice, kindness, and humility are good traits." Then practice them. God says that he will be pleased.

"But should I take this job? Should I marry that man? Should I move to St. Louis? I only want to do God's will."

God wants what is best for you and best for those whose lives yours touches. Ask what is right. Ask what is needed to be done. Ask what will help, not hurt. Ask what will make you a better person. Ask what fulfills you and gives you the sense of realizing a bit more of yourself as a person. Answers to those kinds of questions will indicate what God's will is for your life. He wants the best for you, just as you want the best for those you love.

Do I discount prayer, reading the Bible, going to church, or seeking counsel from a minister? On the contrary, all of those are helpful. After all, how does God get in touch with us except through prayer, his Word, or the church, or the ministry of his messengers? Those are ways of clarifying what is right, needed, helpful, fulfilling.

Sometimes the will of God is quite clear to us. A door opens, and no comparable open door is found. We feel totally good about the decision we have made. But there are other times when all doors seem tightly shut; we can find no latch that will lift. And, on the other hand, occasionally we are confronted by several open doors, any of which appears to be an appropriate way.

The simple truth is that God won't relieve us of the painful but maturing necessity to make decisions. He will help us, but he doesn't do it for us. We don't know the will of God perfectly—not for ourselves, and not for other people. "We walk by faith, not by sight" (2 Cor. 5:7) wrote one of God's men in the Bible.

A great many times we have to get some distance from a perplexing crisis before we can see how God was helping us to make a good decision. We look back and say, "Oh, so that was what that was about! Now I understand why I needed to do what I did."

God doesn't always get his "druthers." If he did, no one would ever be lost. The proper question for the believing person is not, "Why did God do that to me?" but, "Given the present circumstance, what would God have me do?"

4

Our Father Who Art in Heaven

How do you think of God? As Someone on a throne who sulks and pouts when you do not worship him? Do you think you make him unhappy when you do not give him proper attention? Do you fear he may punish you if you neglect to praise him, or believe he will be grateful to you when you go to church or say your prayers?

Do you visualize him as a benevolent grandfather who does not care what you do so long as you enjoy yourself? Do you think of him as a morale builder in crisis, a silent partner whose name adds prestige to our personal endeavors? Is he to you some kind of superman, just like us, only larger and more powerful, filling the measureless reaches of the universe?

It is not easy to think hard, straight thoughts about God. For instance, how do you think of God in terms of time? Before our cities and towns were built, when the dense woodland was dotted with scattered little clearings, God was here. When all the earth lay virgin and unspoiled, God was here.

The seas splashed against our shores and no man heard, but God heard. Before the great ice came down and carved the continent upon which we live God was here. Before that, when this planet was a ball of semimolten matter, with gas spurts exploding miles into the air, God was here. Before earth, sun, and stars there was God. "Before the mountains were brought forth, or ever thou hadst formed the earth and the world, even from everlasting to everlasting, thou art God," (Ps. 90:2, KJV) the psalmist sang.

Think of God as he will be. Our short earthly lives will have been lived, our bodies buried with pathetic pomp and ceremony in the earth from which they came and our souls (for good or ill) gone out on the great adventure—and God will still be here. Our children's children will have forgotten us; the homes we have loved and slaved so hard to pay for will have crumbled into dust—and God will still be here. Our petty achievements will have ceased to be noted; the fortunes we accumulated will have been dissipated; the fame we fought for will be naught; Europe and America will be one with Nineveh and Tyre—and God will still be here.

Around the sun the planet, growing frigid, will move on; and men at last will cease to be, since life of any sort can no longer exist; and the earth will be as the moon is now, and God will still be. The material universe will at last run down, and subside into the nothingness out of which it was made, and God will still be. Only God will be, plus those things which have his nature, among them your spirit and mine.

It is not simple to speak meaningfully of God, for he is God, not just man blown up to universe-size. Men have dared to contemplate him in terms of space. One walks into the night and above are worlds upon worlds, galaxies upon galaxies, defying our puny imaginations to grasp the immensity of the space in which they race at incredible speeds, and God is in it all.

5

Why Don't You Strike Him Down?

In his moving poem, "God's Trombones," James Weldon Johnson recoiled at the treachery of Judas betraying Jesus, and appealed to God:

> Oh, look at black-hearted Judas—
> Sneaking through the dark of the Garden—
> Leading his crucifying mob.
> O God!
> Strike him down!
> Why don't you strike him down,
> Before he plants his traitor's kiss
> Upon my Jesus' cheek?

The question is heavy with theological and personal meaning. Why doesn't God act to prevent treachery, violence, and innocent suffering? For the unbeliever the problem of unmerited suffering exists. He sees it happening to others or experiences it himself. But he is not torn by the distress of wondering why God lets it happen, for he does not believe in God. He believes that we are victims of blind, uncaring chance.

But the believer has a greater burden. Not only does he suffer, or witness the suffering of another, but he is compelled to ask why God lets it happen. Believing that God is both all-powerful and all-loving, how can he accept undeserved pain and grief?

He may decide that evil really does not exist, that it is only an illusion. But if sickness and death are not real, then the illusion that they are real is real! We see these things happen to good people and we wonder why.

Others, believing in a God of justice, conclude that whatever happens serves God's purpose in some mysterious way. Whether they say, "Allah has spoken," or "This is the Lord's will," the verdict is the same. On this line of reasoning God has the world under his control. He made it, and it is inconceivable that he would have made an evil world. Therefore, no matter how grievous the occasion, they must say that it is God's will.

That view of God's relationship with us puts responsibility for terrible crimes on him. If a child is savagely attacked by a mentally defective rapist shall we say, "God's will is done; praise the Lord!"? Should we have asked the six million Jews (and the Christians among them, too) to intone, "God's will is done" as they stumbled into Hitler's gas chambers?

Nor does it help any to argue that there really are no innocent persons and that whatever bad happens to us, therefore, is the punishment of a just God. That sort of theological view simply cannot be respected by a person who thinks much. Do note that there is a profound difference between saying that we are punished for and by our sins, and saying that we can equate the measure of freedom from ills that afflict people with the degree of being "right with God."

All of us know persons victimized by unspeakable calamity. Shall we suspect them of some especially repugnant form of moral evil for which God is "getting even"? The very suggestion is detestable.

Job's comforters espoused that doctrine. They were satisfied that Job was guilty of some blackhearted sin, kept secret to make it appear that he was a good man. How else explain his suffering? Surely God, Maker and Ruler of heaven and earth, would not permit such suffering if Job did not deserve it. Job, having been taught the same theology as his friends believed, but knowing that he was not guilty, could only conclude that God had wronged him.

The point the book of Job makes is that undeserved and inexplicable suffering does exist in our world. One who decides to believe in God must confess that there is mystery in much of human experience. If God is God, we cannot understand him. Any "god" we can explain is an idol, not the Almighty God of the Bible.

How, then, can we be sure of anything about God? How can we say so confidently that he does not do injustice? We say so on the basis of our confidence in the experience of God's people as reported in the Bible, as well as confidence in our own personal experience with God. We put our trust in the claim that God is love.

But if he is love, why does he permit evil to happen unjustly to good and innocent people? One can argue that suffering is permitted as a test of the righteous person's faith. That interpretation has a certain biblical precedence, but it has problems, too.

Why does God need to "test" us? Doesn't he already know our limits? Moreover, what of the rights of the victim who may lose his life in the test? If God takes my child's life to test my faith, what does that say about God's disregard of my child's right to live? That explanation doesn't help me much.

Or one can argue from Scripture that suffering is meant to teach us. The disciplinary nature of hardship is a familiar theme, and it has merit. Some of us have to learn the hard way. No doubt even undeserved suffering can be a great teacher. But that explanation leaves me uneasy, too, because the victims of innocent suffering too often never get a chance to use any knowledge they might have gained from the experience. They are dead.

So we are back to mystery. Johnson's cry to God haunts us: "Why don't you strike him down,/Before he plants his traitor's kiss upon my Jesus' cheek?"

Jesus is mankind's prime example of one unjustly wronged. God could have prevented it. Jesus himself said that his Father would send legions of angels to deliver him if he asked. But he wouldn't do that, and the world stands in awe before the power of his cross to move men and women to repentance and to inspire them to live an unselfish and godly life.

Perhaps Jesus' undeserved death is the clue. Suppose that there is no satisfactory explanation of why these things happen, but there is always the possibility that they may be turned to positive good. By the alchemy of trusting love, we have God's help in transforming tragedy into blessing.

6

We Might Not Like Heaven

I have been hearing sermons about heaven all my life, and never once have I heard it suggested from a pulpit that some people might not like it. Everybody talks as if heaven is life's most desirable destination. If we wish to pay the ultimate compliment we say, "heavenly."

The Bible's vivid imagery of heavenly bliss strengthens the fainthearted and consoles the grief-stricken. Figurative language about streets of gold, walls studded with precious stones, and gates of genuine pearl, reflects the inspired writer's effort to describe the indescribable. We know that "everybody talkin' 'bout heaven ain't going there," but we can't imagine anybody not wanting to.

We take it for granted that we, of all people, would feel right at home in heaven. We come to church and pray, ever so piously, "Thy kingdom come. Thy will be done in earth, as it is in heaven" (Matt. 6:10, KJV). Did we ever stop to ask, "I wonder how it is done in heaven?" Would we really like to have things here the way they are in heaven? I doubt that we could get unanimous consent on that proposition. And it would not surprise me if some of the people who pray the prayer most fervently turned out to be the unhappiest of all if it came to pass.

A prominent religious leader, noted for sharp criticism of folks who dared to disagree with his theology, died. They gave him an impressive funeral; he was eulogized and editorialized. But one man who knew him well said, "Dear Dr. So-and-So is dead. Gone to heaven, I'm sure. But he ain't gonna like God."

Not everybody would like heaven. Some do not have the

nature for it, could not stand the heavenly life. They would be as much out of place in God's presence as the proverbial pig in a parlor. Heaven would surely be hell for some people. Would an illiterate enjoy confinement to a library, especially one without picture books? Would a hard rock music fan be apt to sit enraptured while a symphony orchestra performed Beethoven's Ninth? Would a moral degenerate feel comfortable in a community of ascetics?

One of my favorite authors, C. S. Lewis, wrote a little fantasy about heaven and hell, *The Great Divorce*. A man finds himself in a line of people waiting at a bus stop on a street corner in hell. Only they don't call it hell. It is a great, gray city, with run-down shops, murky weather, and dirty streets running endless miles. The streets appear to be uninhabited, because the residents of the gray city are so selfish and hateful that they continually move farther out.

In time the bus draws up, and after much pushing and shoving, cursing and bickering, the passengers all pile on. Soon the bus is flying through space and at last lands in a wide expanse of green. This turns out to be heaven, a strikingly beautiful place with green lawns, brilliant light, sounds of music and laughter, and persons who look solid, in contrast to the ghostly transparency of the bus passengers.

As the story unfolded, every one of the bus passengers, with one exception, decided he did not want to be a solid person at all. Each preferred to go back to the gray city. A woman, indignant because of the riffraff she had been forced to associate with in the gray city, had made the trip to get away from them, and when she found she could not, she turned back. A businessman met a former employee in the city of solid people and felt much too good for him. He turned back to the bus because, as he put it, "I came here to get my rights, see?"

A cynical ghost wasn't impressed with anything—not even heaven—because he had been everywhere already. This was just another park to him. A dwarf-size man with a chain around his neck was led by a tall figure who was an actor. The small man let the actor do his talking for him, never was himself, but was always pretending, always represented by the actor.

A bishop was in the gray city because he had no real faith, only an intellectual statement of his religion. He could not be humble enough to receive help so that he could stay in the solid state. Besides, he said, he had to get back to the gray city to read a paper before a theological society.

Lewis enjoyed poking fun at stuffed shirts, especially if they were religious stuffed shirts. He claimed no new revelation about heaven and hell. He only raised the issue that people who aren't at home with God here in this life probably won't want to be with him in the next.

7

Our Times Are in His Hands

In such a convulsive era as ours the simple affirmations of faith in God expressed throughout the Bible are a source of steadying strength. Consider Psalm 31:15: "My times are in thy hand." If you believe that, you can face the future with confidence and hope.

Verse 5 of this psalm was repeated by our Lord as he was dying on the cross: "Into thy hands I commend my spirit" (Luke 23:46, KJV). It is said that this verse was taught to every Jewish child by his parents to be said when he went to sleep at night, as our children are taught to say, "Now I lay me down to sleep...."

How fitting that Jesus brought the verse up out of the recesses of childhood memories as he began to slip into the sleep of death. It was a statement of faith. He knew that all of hell's power could not wrench him from his Father's care. He believed this about his followers, too. Of them he once said: "No one is able to snatch them out of my Father's hand" (John 10:29).

Do we believe this? Dare we believe that no matter what comes our lives are held securely in the loving grasp of Almighty God our heavenly Father? The apostle Paul believed it. Recall how he expressed it: "Nothing in all creation ... can separate us from the love of God in Christ Jesus our Lord" (Rom. 8:39, NEB).

Now that is a far different thing from the bland and shallow notion that loving God provides immunity from hurt. Paul was not naive. His own experience had exploded that myth, even if nothing else did. Life could be hazardous, frustrating, lonely, and frighteningly painful. But God held him firmly in his hands. Nothing separated him from the assurance that God loved him.

It is good to have the personal testimony of a man like Paul. But his is not the only witness that might be summoned. Multitudes would stand beside him to confirm his claim. We are in God's hands, they would say. Perhaps you are one of those who has reason to know that you are in his care.

To be assured of this is comforting, of course, but it can also be disturbing. There are times when it would be less upsetting to suppose that God knows nothing of what we are and do than to have to believe that he knows everything. We do not cling to the belief that our lives are in his hands because we are weak and need a security blanket. We believe it because of the witness of the Bible verified in our own experience.

There are times when it would be easier not to believe it. Job, the Old Testament's towering figure of man's suffering, came to a day when he had "had it" with God's being concerned in his affairs. "Why don't you let me alone? Have you not enough to do to run the universe without bothering about me? Let me die in peace," he cried in rebellion. Who has never known such a mood may never have experienced the depths of life.

The same awe over God's interest in us as persons is expressed in the beautiful words of another psalm: "Whither shall I go from thy Spirit? or whither shall I flee from thy presence? ... If I take the wings of the morning, and dwell in the uttermost parts of the sea; Even there shall thy hand lead me, and thy right hand shall hold me" (Ps. 139:7,9-10, KJV). That is comforting only if you are not trying to run away!

As the letter to the Hebrews (10:31) says: "It is a fearful thing to fall into the hands of the living God." That doesn't sound soft and weak, does it?

Our world is scared, and we are often puzzled, frightened citizens of it. There are many weighty questions which we cannot answer: the cause of suffering, the persistence of evil, the inability of man to live with his fellowman on this globe where all are under the shadow of death and where the prospect of extinction is a live option.

But against the folly and lovelessness of man God casts his loving concern. Our hope for the future is in him.

II

Do You Believe?

1

Laura, five, and Carole, nine, were discussing the Easter bunny as they rode along in the back seat of our car. Carole said she didn't believe in the Easter bunny. Laura called up to the front seat, "Grandma, do you believe in the Easter bunny?"

"No," Marion answered, "I don't."

"Do you believe in the Easter bunny, Pop?" she asked me.

Being eldest and wisest of several theologians in our family, I took it upon myself to lecture on the origins and meanings of the Easter bunny. It would have been a dilly, but I only got a couple of sentences in when Laura, sensing where that was going, interrupted: "Do you believe? That's all I want to know."

The question strikes me as terribly important. Do you believe? Don't give me a dissertation. It is not that learning is necessarily a barrier to faith. At least I hope not, for if it is, I have wasted a lot of years. Faith needs to be informed. Some things I don't believe simply because I cannot, knowing what I know. The Easter bunny is a case in point. But I must admit also that there are occasions when intellectualizing an issue is a way to avoid a decision about it.

Do you believe in justice?" someone asks me.

"Well, now," I reply, "that's an interesting question. Do you know the root of the biblical word for justice? Let me tell you how the concept is developed in Scripture, Old Testament and New. After that, I think it might be helpful if we inquired into the Greek and Roman understanding of justice, for we are inheritors of those cultures, too."

The inquirer's rising impatience finally erupts. "Do you, or do you not, believe in justice? That's all I want to know." I think it is a fair question.

When our Lord appeared to his disciples after his resurrection one of them, Thomas, was missing from the group. I have often wondered why he wasn't there. Perhaps Thomas was something of a loner, needing time alone to do his grief work. I could honor that. In any case, he had been absent when, according to John's Gospel, the risen Lord appeared among the disciples in the place where they were hiding in fear. Later when they told Thomas the incredible news, Thomas said he simply could not believe it unless he had proof.

Eight days later the Lord appeared again in their midst. Thomas was present. Christ showed Thomas his nail-scarred hands and wounded side, invited him to come and see and touch, and said "be not faithless, but believing." Honest Thomas cried out in wondering adoration, "My Lord and my God!" (John 20:27-28, KJV).

Thomas would tell you what he thought, no shilly-shallying, no dissembling. "Do you believe in the resurrection?" someone might have asked him before he met the risen Christ. "No," he would have said, "I do not." Asked the same question after he met him, Thomas would have said with equal conviction, "Yes, I believe, for I have seen and touched." In neither case would he have been likely to launch into a lengthy discourse on the implausibility or plausibility of resurrection.

It is possible I will be misunderstood as recommending an unexamined, unquestioning submission to dogma. "Just believe; don't ask questions," someone may read. I hope not, for just the opposite is what I believe. An unexamined faith is not faith at all, but credulity. However, there comes a time, if you have anything to say, to say it. Some of us seem so modest about our convictions that we would be embarrassed to give an inquirer the time of day. We would be much more comfortable delivering a lecture on the daily rotation of the earth.

As chaplain on a college campus I am fortunate to spend my time with intellectuals. How we love to do our intellectual thing! And we are very good at it, let me tell you. Often our language games make me think of Eric Hoffer's contemptuous phrase, "ineffectual men of words."

Lately, however, I've been sitting through some enjoyable seminars on values with colleagues and students. How refreshing it has been to hear someone say, "This is the way it is with me. This I believe."

I would love to have you tell me what you believe in. However, confessing one's faith ought not be the end of conversation with another, but the beginning. It need not be the end unless one's confession is in the form of an unquestionable and unchallengeable dogmatic. In that case it is not confession, but an attempt at coercion. Nobody needs to take that from anybody. Still, my five-year-old granddaughter asked the right question: "Do you believe? That's all I want to know."

2

Share Your Faith; Don't Sell Your Soul

Gospel is a beautiful, musical word in Greek. Transliterated into English, it looks like this: *Euangelion.* There is scarcely a more basic word in Christian vocabulary. From it are derived *evangelism* and *evangelist,* to name only two.

Euangelion was not exclusively a religious term. Sometimes it referred to announcement of a crucial military victory or the end of a catastrophic event. "Something wonderful has happened and everyone will want to know" is the spirit of this word. *Euangelion* is special edition stuff.

Evangelism is the Christian's primary vocation. He has no more important business than to announce the good news. Something so life-altering has happened that he must give everyone who wants it an opportunity to know.

Unfortunately, however, modern evangelism does not always come across as good news. Often it oppresses and dehumanizes victims of overzealous evangelists more intent upon making converts than reporting the liberating acts of God in Christ.

The irony of our humanity is that the best things about us are most easily corrupted. Evangelism is a prime example. Zeal to share what is vital to us often becomes an overbearing disregard of another's religious experience or feelings. The difference between an evangelist and a headhunter is constant vigil over personal attitudes and spirit.

One danger inherent in zealous evangelism is the possible use of manipulative, redundant tricks to bring people to the decision we are after. "Techniques of evangelism" comes close to a contradiction in terms, for it suggests that if you know which buttons to push in another's personality, you can break down his free choice to say yes or no. It may be good salesmanship in the marketplace, but it is poor evangelism. Jesus refused to turn stones into bread or jump from the Temple to gain disciples.

A second danger is misrepresentation. In our zeal to make an impressive case, we may claim more than we know, or dramatize our own experience in such a way that it becomes a caricature. Integrity in evangelism demands not only living the faith we tell others about, but also not getting so carried away with the announcement that we distort the message we announce.

A third danger is spiritual molestation. We use pressing, coercive tactics. In the name of the gentle Christ, we ride roughshod over others, using our Bible to club them into submission to our interpretation of God's message.

Matthew's Gospel repeats Isaiah's prophecy in a beautiful description of Jesus: "He will not wrangle or cry aloud,/nor will anyone hear his voice in the streets;/he will not break a bruised reed/or quench a smoldering wick" (Matt. 12:20, RSV). The picture is of one so sensitive to the rights of others that he would never take advantage of them, even for the sake of a righteous cause.

A fourth danger is condescension, the tendency to say, "I belong to the spiritually elite; believe as I do or it's too bad for you."

The issue turns upon our understanding of *euangelion,* you see. If evangelism is the announcement of good news and not the effort to make other people believe and behave as we do, then we will not need to manipulate, misrepresent, coerce, or condescend. Evangelism becomes, then, not a way of meeting our need to make others conform to us, but a way of telling others something wonderful has happened.

How then evangelize?

First, by living the faith. Wrote C. H. Spurgeon, prince of

evangelists, "The serene, silent beauty of a holy life is the most powerful spiritual force on earth."

Second, maintain a reverent respect for the right of people to be different. Respect them if they do not agree with you.

Third, trust the Spirit. If God had wanted to save people by tricking them, beating them into submission, or scaring them into heaven, he would have done it long since. Instead, he delivered his message through the cross and the resurrection.

3

Choosing the Narrow Way

An ancient church manual called the *Didache,* written in the second century AD, begins with a simple but sweeping declaration: "There are two ways, one of life and one of death, and there is a great difference between the two ways."

We find that hard to believe. Worse, it offends us. Such narrow and definitive language does not suit the modern mood. We prefer to think that there are many ways, all equally valid, and that as long as you are sincere it doesn't matter which one you take. If you really think it doesn't matter, try going south by driving in the northbound lane.

Floundering about in the sea of ambiguity until it becomes a natural habitat, we do not realize how much we are at odds with the wisdom of the ages. Joshua said to the children of Israel: "Choose you this day whom ye will serve, . . . but as for me and my house, we will serve the Lord" (Josh. 24:15, KJV).

Do You Believe? / 35

Jeremiah the prophet told his people: "These are the words of the Lord: 'I offer you now a choice between the way of life and the way of death.'"

When we come to Jesus in the New Testament, we find him no less positive about the need to make the choices which life demands: "Enter by the narrow gate; for the gate is wide and the way is easy that leads to destruction, and those who enter by it are many. For the gate is narrow and the way is hard that leads to life, and those who find it are few" (Matt. 7:13-14, RSV).

If the sharp edges of those words had not been worn smooth by rolling off pulpits, they would prick us—two gates, two ways, two destinies. The one, taken by many because it is the path of least resistance, is deadly. The other, taken by few because it restricts one's choices and offers a specific goal, is life-giving.

Taking the broad way seems to make the painful act of choice-making unnecessary. We choose not to choose, or so we imagine, refusing to realize that not choosing is itself a choice.

The broad way looks enticing. Who wants to be restricted to a narrow road when the wide and spacious one is available? Indeed, would it not be ideal to have no road at all? In that case there would be no limitations—no curbs, no markers, no signs, no right and wrong ways, and no arrival or departure.

In the desert we could drive in whatever direction suited our fancy. Drive east for an hour or so. If the sun got in our eyes, we could drive west for a while, or maybe north for a couple of hours. It wouldn't matter, for all directions are really the same. Besides, the ride is what counts, not where you are going.

Our times are peopled by folks driving aimlessly across the desert. These nomads occasionally stumble upon an oasis, but mostly they just drive. Sometimes they find that they have been chasing mirages. If that is freedom, welcome to it.

The narrow road has its disadvantages, to be sure. It is restrictive. You can't take off in all directions if you are going to take the narrow road. And you run the risk that it may send you down some little out-of-the-way path that ends in triviality or irrelevancy, and you might miss the main road without ever knowing it.

Or being on the narrow road may encourage elitism, which prides itself on being separated from the *hoi polloi*. Or it may foster paranoia or a persecution complex, so we make a career out of rehearsing all it costs us to travel the narrow way. Or it may make us judgmental and tight-lipped about everybody who chooses another road.

But the narrow road has its advantages, too. It assures the channeling of energies. The narrow road requires a certain direction. We can't wander aimlessly on a one-way street.

Would you release the power in gasoline? Confine it. Would you harness the power of a river? Send it down between the confines of a turbine. Take away its restrictions and it becomes a swamp. Jesus eloquently expressed the wisdom of the ages: "The road that leads to life is narrow" (Matt. 7:14).

As Jesus faced the cross, he consciously chose the way that ended at Golgotha. The Gospels say it plainly: "He stedfastly set his face to go to Jerusalem" (Luke 9:51). He, too, had to make a choice. He opted for the narrow road that led to Calvary. Because he did he experienced the resurrection.

4

What Would I Die For?

Some of us in the university where I serve as chaplain were involved in a "values seminar" with students. When asked to speak eight minutes on my personal values, I imagined that I was in an overloaded boat in the middle of the ocean and it was sinking. What would I throw overboard and what would I keep to the very end? Those things, I decided, were my real values, and they evened out at ten.

First, my relationship with God is crucial. If it turns out to be a no-God universe, I shall have really missed it. Second is relationship with people—family, friends, people I have never seen but have tried to help and bless. Third is justice, a passion for fairness for all persons, including myself, and shame if I help perpetrate injustice toward any person.

Fourth is integrity, for without it life is not worth living. The director of NASA was asked, "What personal qualities do you consider responsible for success among scientists and engineers who have made the U.S. space program so effective?" He replied, "What I look for in a man ... is first high integrity. That in itself won't do the job, but without it, no matter how brilliant he is, a man won't be capable of working with a program like ours."

Fifth on my list is loyalty, which has to do with integrity, to be sure, but is something special to me. Loyalty prods me to do what I have agreed to do even if it inconveniences or pains me. Sixth is ambition, to fulfill as much of my potential as I can within the limits of my years and other values.

Seventh is my heritage, which is white Anglo-Saxon Protestant, and which I believe has contributed much to the human race. No race is without its history of exploitation and cruelty to others. While I deplore the evil that my ancestors inflicted upon others, I also value what they contributed to Western civilization.

Eighth is freedom to live relatively free of coercion. Ninth is inquisitiveness, dissatisfaction with what I already know, a consuming need to go on learning. Tenth and last is the ability to make my own way in the world and not be a burden on my family or society. I have a great need to be self-supporting, and value highly my ability to carry my share of the load and more.

Those were the values I claimed to college students. Perhaps you would state yours differently. God bless you, go to it. The silence about values is what ought to disturb us. Too long we have been silent in our homes and classrooms about the values which we attach to the multitude of experiences to which modern man is exposed.

"There is no such thing as value-free education," the Danforth Foundation Report said recently. If the college does not teach values they will be taught in other ways. For instance, a study made some time ago revealed that high school graduates have on the average spent 15,000 hours of their lives in front of the television but only 11,000 hours in formal schooling. More significantly, their personal values and preferences have been subjected to exposure to 640,000 commercials.

A distinguished American scholar has said that "We might ... leave higher education to its intellectual values exclusively were it not for one fact. That fact is the present condition of Western man ... for a hundred years now this condition has drawn mounting concern from its most perceptive observers. ... Diagnoses and prognoses differ widely in detail, but on these two points there is concert: the sickness is acute, and its locus is in the realm of values."

5

The Capacity to Endure Uncertainty

John Finley of Harvard defined maturity as "the capacity to endure uncertainty." If that be so, this is not a mature time—if any ever was—for our age is impatient with ambiguity. We require simple, clear-cut answers. "Just give me the bottom line," is the motto of the successful decision maker.

We act as though we ought to be able to explain God Almighty himself in a *Reader's Digest* piece no more than five pages long. Of course, it should be written in two-syllable words put in sentences of no more than ten words. Better still would be to explain God with a series of photographs, briefly captioned.

It is one of the mysteries that the more religious we become the less patient and comfortable we are prone to be with the heart of religion, namely, the mystery of God. One would suppose that as one draws closer to the Infinite one would be progressively overwhelmed by the awesomeness of the experience.

That is precisely what happened to the prophet Isaiah. Encountering the Divine was literally indescribable. All he could do was to use the vehicle of ordinary language to communicate an extraordinary experience. Words failed him; they were inadequate, no matter how beautiful they were. The only appropriate response he could make was the cry, "Woe is me, ... I am a man of unclean lips" (Isa. 6:5, KJV).

The wisest, the purest, the most dedicated among us have stammering tongues when they speak God's name. They stammer precisely because they are wise, pure, and dedicated. They know enough to know that they do not know. They do not bawl the name of God like a popcorn vendor at the stadium.

As a matter of fact, the observation about the mystery of God may be generalized to include all reality. We know such an infinitesimal part of the whole of anything. Stephen Bayne's comment about this is worth reporting: "Part of every man's education, and assuredly part of every Christian education, ought certainly to be an education in ignorance."

The classic statement of the necessity to live with uncertainty is found in Paul's immortal song of love, 1 Corinthians 13: "For we know in part, and we prophesy in part" (v. 9, KJV). People who insist on knowing and prophesying in full suggest, whether they intend to do so or not, that they have out-distanced the apostle in spiritual maturity.

"Now we see only baffling reflections in a mirror" (v. 12), Paul wrote. One day, he said, we shall turn around and look Reality in the face. Until then we shall have to be content with the reflections of it. Faith exists as a lively confidence that the reflections are images of a Reality we do not now see.

Was Paul implying that faith is nothing more than a pious hope, a creation of the imagination which is unable to bear looking into the mirror and seeing nothing? By no means. We have glimpsed the Reality. We *do* know in part. But to suggest that the little we know of God is all there is to know is the ultimate arrogance. We walk by faith, not by sight.

That is a hard doctrine. We much prefer walking by sight. We want our preachers to reassure us that there are no mysteries to trouble the mind. We like being told, "Only believe." Crowds follow the man or woman who announces confidently, "Come, hear the answer. Come, find certainty. You do not have to be worried by ambiguity. It's all very simple: one, two, three."

What is tantalizing about such doctrine is that it has a certain biblical plausibility. The Bible does say: "You will seek me and will find me when you seek me with all your heart" (Jer. 29:13,

KJV). Jesus did say, "Come unto me, ... and I will give you rest.... Learn of me, ... and ye shall find rest unto your souls" (Matt. 11:28-29, KJV).

But in our need to oversimplify and dispel all mystery we leap from the promise of God's presence and comfort to the conclusion which we ourselves want, namely, that we may be free from the need to live in faith. If we just had all the answers, it would make life much more pleasant.

In order to gain such a state of bliss we trade the mystery for cheap nostrums. We refuse to acknowledge the questions, or we give them shallow answers. Ignorance may be bliss, but it is not virtue. If the options are avoidance of the pain of living with uncertainty, dissonance, and contradiction, or accepting and living with them in faith, I choose the latter.

Kierkegaard put it plainly when he said that we are called to live at that perilous midpoint equidistant between security and despair. Neither absolute security nor black despair is possible for the person who believes in God. That is not a popular word at this time, for we are desperate for security. Anyone who promises it can get rich quickly. We pay handsomely for the spiritual analgesic.

But Jesus found a cross, Paul a headsman's axe, Stephen a lynch mob. Still they were secure, safe in the confidence that God is God, and that he is a loving Father. And that is quite enough.

6

Learning to Let Go

Who is more miserable, the person who never risks making friends, or the one so insecure that he cannot bear to let them come and go? The first never trusts himself to accept another's genuine caring. The other cannot give thanks for the gift he has had when it must be relinquished, either temporarily or forever.

Those related to a college community have an annual reminder that learning to let people go is an important part of the curriculum of life. Graduation is letting students go so that, at their will, the college may have them back in a new relationship.

Letting go is an art, the first part of which is realizing that you have to. In this world, at least, no relationship is permanent. "Till death do us part" is a promise many people still manage to keep, yet even that is provisional—till death.

All relationships are continually altered by what life does to us. One learns to accept the alterations, finding meaning in them, or one becomes miserable and bitter. Only when we open our hands to let go what we have to give up will they be positioned to receive other gifts.

Letting go is not an act of disloyalty. Some people never get over feeling guilty about leaving, do not know how to say good-bye. And some people never let another say good-bye without laying a load of guilt on him for saying it. People who do that are dealing with their own inadequacies. The parent is afraid the child will grow up and not need the parent. The teacher is afraid his pupil will go beyond him. The friend fears his friend may no longer need him. The mature person neither uses guilt to hold on to relationships nor allows it to be used on him when it is clearly the time to go.

Letting go takes both courage and faith. One cannot be sure of a safe landing. The trapeze artist offers a metaphor of all human relationship. Every person swings somewhat perilously on a flying trapeze. A moment comes when you simply must take your courage in your hands and let go. You have to release your grip, confident that you will be caught by other strong hands. If you cannot, you may as well climb down.

With courage, trust is required. You have to believe that you are going to be caught as you hang there suspended in midair. People with a low trust factor have a hard time letting go. They are sure disaster awaits them if they do.

But if we trust life, trust ourselves, trust God, there is always a way. We may never have the same things we had and were compelled by the process of living to surrender, but there are other things. Despite irretrievable losses, security and beauty are offered elsewhere if our hands are open to receive.

7

To Be a Redemptive Minority

If you read the Bible much, you will conclude that the Almighty has known all along that if this world is changed it will be because of a dedicated minority. Somebody must be willing to be different, to care more, give more, sacrifice more, work harder, and, if necessary, die.

It is the meaning of the Bible. God chose a people. He elected them. They misread their election to mean special privilege. He meant it to be special service. They were called to be a redemptive minority.

Jesus understood God's call. Jesus did not despise popularity, but he understood that it may not be rightly bought at the price of fidelity to God. He saw his personal following dwindle until he said one day to the twelve disciples, "Will you also go away?" (John 6:67, RSV).

Jesus instilled in the lives of his few followers the commitment to serve as a redemptive minority. He called them "leaven" and "salt." A little bit of either does a lot. He warned them that a redemptive minority would see hard times. "You will be hated by all for my name's sake" (Matt. 10:22, RSV), he said.

Paul saw it, too. Writing to some Christian friends, he told them that they were like lights in a darkened world, that they stood amidst a crooked and perverse generation, holding forth the word of life. Paul said nothing to make one believe that in a little time everybody would come to join the Christians, filling the world with a blaze of God's glory.

It is curious and unfortunate that we find the lesson hard to learn. We don't like to be alone. It gets harder and harder to buck the world. It is a sore temptation to say, "If you can't lick 'em, join 'em!" The hazards of the minority are so great that one wonders if God doesn't often get weary of both majority and minority.

Evil is such an insidious thing that it corrupts even our efforts to do good. At no place is this more evident than in the reactions of most minorities, even those dedicated to God's service. For one thing, they get to feeling sorry for themselves. Self-pity, a luxury we can ill afford, is well-nigh a vocational hazard for a minority group. Like Elijah of old, we imagine ourselves to be the only true and faithful people left. Elijah, a good and brave man, got bogged down in self-pity. He was suffering from battle fatigue in his struggle with paganism. He needed to be told that there were seven thousand others who had not bowed the knee to Baal.

Harsh judgmentalism is a common pitfall. Why is it that so many "good" people are thin-lipped and humorless? What is there about us that dries up all the joy in us when we become too aware of being different? It is almost as if we look upon the merry majority and secretly envy its carefree behavior. We seem to be saying: "Go ahead, have your fun. You'll catch it later in hell, and then we'll see who has the last laugh!"

Pride, haughtiness, and exclusiveness are special temptations, although they are shared by the human race, of course. But are they not often a consolation prize for coming out at the small end of the horn? We say, "We are the people of God, the elite; we alone have the truth."

Withdrawal, disengagement, retreat tempts the minority. If we cannot win the world to our view, we shall leave it. We won't be intimidated by its power.

How can we deal with the hazards of the minority? Well, forewarned is sometimes forearmed. Avoid these very temptations. Remember that God has chosen a minority willing to love, serve, and patiently endure to redeem the rest of the human family.

III

A Time to Laugh

1

"There is a time to weep, and a time to laugh" (3:4, KJV), says Ecclesiastes. This Old Testament writer, who called himself the Preacher, contended that "To every thing there is a season" (3:1, KJV). I am glad he included laughter.

Religious people should remember that laughter is as much a part of God's order as is prayer. Jesus is our best example here, as everywhere. He who wept over Jerusalem also enjoyed himself so thoroughly at the houses of his friends that it was a scandal to pious folk who mistook his gaiety for debauchery. They suspected that he was a winebibber and a glutton. How sad that they should have missed so much!

Do we? Is the joy of life which erupts into infectious laughter missing from our religion? Too bad. The early Christians, like their Lord, knew that there was a time to weep but also a time to laugh. "The church is the one thing that always rejoices," was the way a third-century writer described it.

St. Francis of Assisi, God's troubadour and friend of birds and animals, filled with joy and affectionate trust, would be good medicine for many pious souls. Listen to him.

> I love my God and he loves me, merrily
> I feel his kisses in the breeze,

> And so I carve his name on trees—why not?
> Ten thousand years misunderstood
> He needs my laughter in the wood—a lot!

Do not be one of those dull souls who supposes that being a Christian is always a matter of dead seriousness and that God is offended by the sound of laughter. That was the way many pious people of Jesus' day thought about God. They were very careful lest they offend him with a little frivolity. They were careful to dress just right, walk just right, talk just right, keeping all the multitudinous regulations of their religion with meticulous care. What a miserable existence!

A look at the life of Jesus shows why people found his personality irresistible. He once described his relationship with life as a wedding reception where everyone is filled with good wishes and buoyant enthusiasm. How can a person of goodwill be churlish at a wedding party?

His happiness corresponded to the universal law that joy comes from self-forgetfulness. The happiest people are the very people who are most interested in other people and are doing most for them. The surest recipe for a joyless, meaningless life is to look at yourself constantly and interpret all reality in terms of how it affects you. Jesus said simply that we find our lives by losing them. It is so simple that we will not take it seriously, yet it is life's profoundest lesson.

Further, the joy of Jesus was the product of his unwavering faith in God his Father. Genuine laughter—not the bitter, cynical wisecrack or the vulgarity which is a substitute for real humor—arises out of a sense of well-being. Such a sense can come only from confidence in the ultimate trustworthiness of life. It comes, in short, from faith in God.

Leslie Weatherhead once put this plainly: "The opposite of joy," he said, "is not sorrow. It is unbelief." It ought not to surprise us, then, that the Christian should laugh and sing; after all, he has a great deal to laugh about. As George Fox, the great Quaker, put it, the Christian understands that though there is an ocean of darkness and death, there is also an ocean of light and love which flows over the ocean of darkness.

2

How to Remain Reasonably Sane

In *The Psychological Society,* Martin Gross describes us as "the most anxious, emotionally insecure and analyzed population in the history of man." I am afraid he is right. "We live in a civilization in which, as never before, man is preoccupied with Self," Gross observes.

Such preoccupation provides the clue to our endemic anxiety and insecurity. Everyone seems intensely concerned with discovering his own elusive "identity." "I Gotta Be Me," a pop song title goes. We go about interpreting all reality as though we were the center of it, searching relentlessly for the Holy Grail of "Who am I?" Have we forgotten (Did we ever learn?) that "[he] whosoever will save his life shall lose it?" (Matt. 16:25, KJV).

If I interpret all reality in terms of how I am affected, I can only conclude that much of the time life is either indifferent or hostile to me. Obviously, much of what happens in the world takes no notice of me or of my preferences, and some of the time what happens is to my disadvantage or injury. Shall I conclude that the universe is friendly only when it appears to smile on me?

Thinking only or mainly of myself magnifies the frustrations and aggravates the hurts which unavoidably accompany my humanness. Maybe God does not experience frustration and hurt (although I think he does). In any event, I do. It is one thing to try to avoid the hurts and pains, or to get over them if they are unavoidable. It is quite another thing to operate one's life on the illusion that one is entitled to freedom from pain in order to enjoy perfect happiness and total fulfillment.

If freedom from frustration and pain is the measure of normalcy, we are all abnormal by definition. Nobody has resolved all perplexities, eased all stress, avoided all anxiety or despair.

The first requirement for remaining reasonably sane is to give up the illusion of a right to pain-free and stress-free existence. There is no great virtue in stoicism about pain. I reach for the aspirin when I have a headache. But I would set myself up to be a "sicky" if I allowed myself the insupportable luxury of supposing that constant bliss and unbroken peace of mind are my entitlement.

The second thing I can do to remain reasonably sane is not to act crazy. I can't always control my fantasies. Mine get pretty wild—I have a vivid imagination! I can't always control my feelings, either. But one thing I am in charge of is my behavior. That I am responsible for. I don't think I can excuse shabby or sick behavior on the grounds that the devil made me do it, or that my mother failed to cuddle me enough as a child.

So, if I am having trouble functioning, and if I feel rotten, one place I can begin dealing with myself is at the point of my behavior. What am I doing that perpetuates unhealthy feelings and imaginations? What can I do to restore some measure of normalcy to my behavior patterns? The chances are quite good that if I act responsibly, despite feelings of irresponsibility or inadequacy, I shall discover after a time that my feelings have come around to the positive side.

Most importantly, remaining reasonably sane in this crazy

world is to find for oneself a source of ultimate meaning and reliance—in simple, unambiguous words, to come to terms with God. To be sure, religion itself can be a source of mental illness. Freud erroneously supposed that it always was. He saw patients insane with presumed guilt and concluded that guilt is always a sick response to what one is and has done. He saw people as victims of religious illusion, not as sinners who needed to repent and accept God's grace of forgiveness and newness of life.

Freud did not eliminate sin and guilt. What he did was to take away the one sure resource for dealing adequately with sin and guilt, namely, good news of a loving heavenly Father who forgives and makes us new despite our fallenness, and who enables us to reshape our lives after his likeness.

The country is full of people seeking therapy for their mental and emotional hurts. Many have lost touch with or faith in the power of God's forgiveness of sin. That resource is not seen as an option for them. So what are they to do? If I cannot confess my sin, and if there is no one to forgive and restore me, what am I to do?

In his disturbing book, *Whatever Became of Sin?* Dr. Karl Menninger, a psychiatrist himself, laments the loss of the sense of sin and the possibility of redemption from sin in modern society. He argues that we turned "sin" into "symptom," and says pointedly: "It does little good to repent a symptom, but it may do great harm not to repent a sin."

I don't think that God is to be used as another "cure for whatever ails you." Any time God becomes a utility to us he ceases to be God to us. You can't prescribe "God," or dispense him from a medicine bottle. God won't play games, or be anyone's remedy. But he is God; he does love us; he invites us to trust and love him in return. Doing so keeps people reasonably sane and able to function, even under enormous pressure and stress.

3

Getting to the Breaking Point

Everybody sooner or later reaches the breaking point. That is the place where desperation replaces reason and you feel you cannot go on. Some people get there often, for they live close to it; they may even reside on the edge of the abyss. Others have only heard about it so far, or may have seen it only once in their whole lives. But late or soon, infrequently or often, we all get there.

The apostle Paul got there at least once. He told of it in a letter he wrote to some friends. We call the letter 2 Corinthians, and the reference to this moment of desperation comes at the very beginning of the piece. He said it was something that happened to him—what it was we do not know—while he was in Ephesus.

"We should like you, our brothers, to know something of what we went through in Asia. At that time we were completely overwhelmed, the burden was more than we could bear, in fact, we told ourselves that this was the end. Yet we believe now that we had this experience of coming to the end of our tether that we might learn to trust, not in ourselves, but in God who can raise the dead" (1:8-9, Phillips).

Note carefully the way this godly man described his feelings: "Completely overwhelmed, the burden more than we could bear, ... this was the end." It was no temporary inconvenience, no minor setback. In fact, the best way he could describe it was to say that he had come "to the end of our tether." He was at the end of his rope.

What caused it? We can only guess. Perhaps it was illness.

Maybe it was persecution, for in another letter he wrote, "Did I not fight with beasts at Ephesus?" (1 Cor. 15:32). Perhaps it was the awful sense of complete rejection by the Corinthians themselves, for there had been hard feelings toward him in that church. Nobody really knows, for Paul did not air his troubles much. But we do know that it brought him to the breaking point.

He had discovered in this experience what all of us find out: One quickly exhausts whatever resources one has when a critical situation arises. Sometimes it takes only a split second to bring us face-to-face with matters of ultimate consequence. Then we know how very helpless we are and how very little we can do.

How many are the experiences that bring us to the end of our rope! Some bad and unalterable condition which has to do with job or home or mate or child. Some unruly fear kindled into a consuming flame that will not be quenched, robbing us of sleep and needed strength. Some unmanageable desire which becomes a kind of obsession. Some plaguing habit or attitude which keeps sticking its ugly, grinning face into our consciousness. Some defect of body or mind. Some separation which can never be bridged. Some door forever closed. Some quicksand of despair into which we sink deeper and deeper, despite all our flailing efforts and wailing cries.

Have you never been to the breaking point, the end of your rope? Are you there now? What do you do when you get there?

For one thing, be sure you really are. There is a difference between being at the end of your resources and being merely temporarily inconvenienced. Anybody who listens to people's troubles a good bit knows that there are a lot of folks who start hollering "calf rope" the first time they run into a little trouble.

To be sure, we do not all have the same breaking point. It is therefore dangerous to jump to conclusions about whether people are really having serious trouble or are only enjoying feeling sorry for themselves. God Almighty must have a great deal of patience to put up with our whining and crying for his help every time we get under pressure.

But if you are at the end of your rope you will likely ask for God's help. If you are really there, so will he be. This is to say, when we have done all we can do God's grace will underwrite our efforts and supply what we lack.

Paul believed this. In fact, he said that he had come to believe that the experience was meant to remind him to trust God instead of relying solely upon his own wits.

What this means is that God is no magic wand to be waved, no Aladdin's lamp to be rubbed. "He cooperates with us for good" (Rom. 8:28), as Paul put it in another letter.

He will work with us. He will supply our lack. He will comfort the comfortless, bind up the wounds of the brokenhearted, and supply his grace to those who are at the breaking point.

4

He Forgives As We Forgive

Our Lord said more about forgiveness than he did about many sins that need forgiving—including adultery. It was not that he took such matters lightly, but that he knew refusal to forgive was more destructive than most of the sins we commit against God and each other.

For one thing, refusing to forgive is self-destructive, releasing in us a vicious enemy which eats like cancer at our spirit and often does serious damage even to our physical health.

Concentrating on the wounds we have suffered distracts us from constructive effort, drains our energies from useful channels, pouring them into the futile, self-defeating, stream of bitterness.

More than that, refusing to forgive is a sin against others. When we cry, "I can't get over what he did to me!" what we really mean is, "I'll never let him get over it. I'll punish him the rest of his life." It is also a sin against the innocent who are involved with us: children, parents, friends, business associates, etc. Our lives are inextricably bound together, and we cannot hurt one another individually. Refusing to forgive does not better the lot of the one wronged; it only makes bad matters worse.

Most of all, withholding forgiveness puts one in a precarious position before God. Every time we pray the Lord's Prayer we say something frightening: "Forgive us our debts,/As we also have forgiven our debtors" (Matt. 6:12, RSV). That petition makes two affirmations, that we are under an unpayable obligation to God and can never square accounts but only implore him to absorb our debts, and that we may expect him to do this only as we demonstrate by forgiving that we know what it is to absorb debts.

Our Lord commented on only one of the six petitions of this best-loved prayer, and this is the one. Was it that he realized how hard it is for us to forgive? This is his comment: "For if you forgive men their trespasses, your heavenly Father also will forgive you; but if you do not forgive men their trespasses, neither will your Father forgive your trespasses" (Matt. 6:14-15, RSV).

This is not because God does not want to forgive, but because he cannot. His forgiveness is not conditioned by the need to get him into a forgiving mood. God is love, and forgiveness is his nature. But he cannot give us what we will not have; even God cannot forgive if we will not be forgiven. And we show that we do not want, understand, or appreciate forgiveness when we refuse it to each other. Consider carefully that whoever will not forgive another has destroyed the road over which he himself must travel.

Jesus told a parable when Simon Peter asked about how many times he should forgive one who had sinned against him. Would not seven times be generous? Jesus answered, "Seventy times seven" (Matt. 18:22). That is, indefinitely. And then he told the story of a slave who, having defaulted on a fantastic debt of ten million dollars went to his master and begged and received mercy.

But the same slave then went and seized by the throat a fellow slave who owed him a paltry twenty dollars and demanded payment. Jesus said that when the master learned what had happened he revoked his cancellation of the ten million dollar debt. The point is plain: Do not expect God to forgive your greater debt to him unless you can show that you know what it is to be forgiven by forgiving.

But how does one forgive a hurt that has shattered one's dreams, broken one's sense of trust, and destroyed one's self-confidence? There is no easy answer. We are not talking about condonement, excusing, making light of wrong, acting as if nothing has marred relationships. Forgiveness means each party faces what has been done, each assesses and assumes his part, each resolves to bear the shame and the hurt, and then begins anew.

5

Using Guilt Constructively

Guilt is an old-fashioned word, conjuring up ugly images of self-abasement, anxiety, and depression. People don't want to accept the burden of guilt. It hurts. Guilt can debilitate and immobilize us in hand-wringing self-despising. But guilt can have positive uses.

Only the psychopath never feels guilty, and he does not because he has no moral sense. He may be sorry that he is caught, but he is deterred only by the fear of punitive action, not by the principle of right or wrong. Most people do experience remorse, however, when they fail to meet their own expectations of the right thing to do. Whether such responses are helpful or harmful depends upon the use we make of them.

All of us devise defenses against guilt. We blame circumstances, fate, the times. Edmund, illegitimate son of Gloucester in *King Lear,* says it eloquently: "When we are sick in fortune,—often the surfeit of our own behaviour,—we make guilty of our disasters the sun, the moon, and the stars; as if we were villains by necessity, fools by heavenly compulsion, knaves, thieves, treachers by spherical predominance" (Act I, Scene 2).

Often we blame other people. If our parents had brought us up differently, loved us more, disciplined us more, or less, we would be more mature. The government is to blame. They make crooks of us all. Television has corrupted us. The times are out of joint.

Sometimes we handle guilt by appeasement. We try to "make up" for our feeling of unworthiness by excessive generosity. Once I stood with a family at the grave of their son who had committed suicide, and they said: "One thing we can take comfort in is that we never denied him anything he wanted." I wanted to say, "More's the pity."

We resort to self-righteousness. Self-esteem becomes twisted into holier-than-thou behavior, a self-righteousness mask behind which we hide our self-hatred for wrongdoing.

The flip side of self-righteousness is self-abasement. We atone for our sin by telling ourselves and others "I am no good. I am a rotten, miserable person."

We point the finger at others' flaws. We are so disturbed by what we see in the hidden recesses of our own minds that we feel everyone else must see it, too. Lest they do look and find us out, we call attention to others' miserable parts. "Look at those awful people! See what they do."

A similar form of this behavior is what is sometimes called "reaction formation"—we protest what we fear in ourselves. We give ourselves away when we are forever harping about some particular behavioral problem.

Can guilt feelings ever be constructive? Of course. They are constructive if they are taken to be what they really are—the pain resulting from having wronged our own moral sensibilities.

If I have a physical pain it is foolhardy to ignore it. My body is warning me. The distress signal sent to my brain may be minor—or it may be quite serious—but pain calls for an appropriate response. If it is something that can be cured with minimal adjustment, then that is the thing to do. If it requires radical surgery, it won't help if I ignore it or try minor medication.

Guilt is spiritual pain. The spirit says, "There is something wrong here. You need to look into this, and make some changes." Now, of course, we can get this spiritual pain all out of focus. In that case, we probably need someone whom we trust to say, "You are overreacting. You are making a big thing out of nothing."

It works the other way, too. Sometimes we ignore warning signs of guilt, destroying ourselves in the process. If we are doing that we also need someone whose loving concern we trust to say to us, "You cannot afford to go on ignoring the danger signals of your guilt feelings."

The most constructive use of guilt is confession and acceptance of forgiveness from God. He frees us from the weight of self-praise, self-despising, contempt for others, and other faces of guilt. We can know this only by submitting to the healing which he can perform in our lives.

If these words have any personal meaning for you, get down your Bible and read Psalm 51 and Luke 7:36-50. God helps us to use our spiritual pain constructively.

6

Sources of Joy

There is too little joy. You can find plenty of gaiety, even hilarity, but not an abundance of joy. Joy is not a product that can be manufactured, or induced with amplified sound and black light. Joy is not a product at all. It is a condition, a state of being, emerging like cold spring water from the deep recesses of one's basic character.

Joy is frequently confused with enjoyment, and enjoyment is identified with pleasure. But pleasure is not joy. It is at best a cheap imitation. Many a person is so fed up with his dreary existence that he knocks himself out in a frantic search for some new and satisfying "high."

Haverford College psychology professor Douglas Heath has described this generation as suffering from a "deepening sense of boredom, a kind of malaise." He argues that because of affluence many of us have never experienced real drudgery, hard work, and long hours, and thus have a low tolerance level for what is certainly the everyday existence of most men on the planet. "We want creative, fulfilling and meaningful work which makes an impact." Such expectations eliminate about 90 percent of what is available to be done.

Not only are we unable to endure hard work, but we are victims of excessive stimulation. We humans adapt quickly to new levels of stimulation. Remember how excited you were at the first moon landing, as contrasted with the matter-of-fact acceptance of the last one?

Boredom also results from exhaustion of novelty. People whose interest in life is sustained only by some new experience are playing a self-defeating game. After a while there is nothing left. A youth who "burns himself out" by the time he is eighteen has nothing left to anticipate except some new form of stimulation to kick himself into a higher gear.

Joy arises at a level other than pleasure. Joy is possible only where the capacity to care deeply is nourished. Jesus is mankind's superlative example of caring. Because he cared so deeply he was filled with both joy and sorrow. The two are not alien to one another, but counterparts of caring.

The deeper we feel, the more keenly we experience both joy and sorrow. If we never intend to suffer a deep loss, we must never be made vulnerable by love. And the more people we care for the more often we will know both joy and grief. The saying goes, "He who lives more lives than one, more deaths than one must die." Yes, but he also lives more than one life. And it is worth the price.

God invites us to make our lives a vast communication system with a central registering bell and many sensitive wires stretching out in every direction to others. And the more wires we put out the more often the bell rings in our souls, sounding an alarm or announcing good news. He who dislikes being disturbed by the bell disconnects the wires and sits in silence in his prison self.

In his epistle to the Romans Paul put the matter simply: "Rejoice with them that do rejoice; weep with them that weep" (12:15, KJV). Both are authentic responses to the human situation; both result from caring, and caring is our highest vocation.

Joy is a condition which depends upon the ability to forget oneself, to lose oneself in a cause which claims so much that we no longer are preoccupied with ourselves.

Joy is the satisfaction that comes as a by-product from having found our way in life, from confidence that the road leads somewhere. Jesus knew such joy and promised it to his followers. That confidence enabled him to say the night before his death: "I have spoken thus to you, so that my joy may be in you, and your joy complete" (John 15:11, NEB).

7

Surprised by Joy

The late C. S. Lewis gave his autobiography the engaging title, *Surprised by Joy*. It is the story of his pilgrimage from conventional Christianity into atheism and then back into a fresh, personal confrontation of the reality of God in Christ.

Lewis' experience was suited to his personality. A rational man, he was not stirred by emotional appeals or by church services. He confessed that he disliked the organ most of all musical instruments.

But he read, thought, and discussed Christianity's claims with friends. One day, riding atop a bus, he felt as if he were sitting inside a suit of armor and had to decide whether to keep it on or take it off and make himself vulnerable to the reality which stood ready to invade him.

Lewis went home, got on his knees, and deliberately and consciously took off his "armor." He was not ready yet to believe in Christ, but only to say that he believed in God. He kept at the search. One day it happened. Here are Lewis' words: "I was driven to Shipsnade one sunny morning. When we set out I did not believe that Jesus Christ is the Son of God, and when we reached the zoo I did. Yet I had not exactly spent the journey in thought. Nor in great emotion. . . . It was more like when a man, after a long sleep, still lying motionless in bed, becomes aware that he is now awake."

But what of his search for joy? Did his newfound faith end all his doubts and feelings of emptiness? "To tell you the truth," he writes in conclusion, "the subject (of joy) has lost nearly all interest for me since I became a Christian. . . . I believe that the old stab, the old bittersweet, has come to me as often and as sharply since my conversion as at any time in my life. . . . But I now know that the experience, considered as a state of my own mind, had never had the kind of importance I once gave it."

Lewis' confession of faith has a certain disarming winsomeness, its strong appeal the gentle refusal to make his experience normative. He wants only to make plain what happened to him, not to insist that his is the only way to be apprehended by the reality of Christ.

Two of Jesus' pithy comments on how people enter the kingdom of God come to mind. One is about a farmer plowing a field and unexpectedly turning up a buried treasure. Quickly covering his "find," he goes "in his joy and sells all that he has and buys that field" (Matt. 13:44, RSV). To have the treasure he must own the field, and it is worth everything.

The other vignette describes a pearl merchant, an expert, who spends his life searching for the ultimate pearl of great price. One day he finds it. As did the farmer with his unsought and unexpected find, this merchant gladly exchanged everything he owned to obtain the prize.

In some ways the two characters are alike. Both felt compelled to act upon their discovery. Both had to give up everything, making the object they had found the one value above all.

But the way in which the two are different is as significant as their similarities. One "stumbled" on his find, while the other was a lifelong student of the object of his search.

Perhaps we could be a little more relaxed with each other, and act toward one another with some of the Christian charity we recommend to the world, if we could accept Jesus' own description of the variety of ways in which people "find" the kingdom of God. One of our idolatries is to absolutize our own understanding of God, rather than worshiping the God who refuses to be limited to our experience.

To deny that God may be found except as we find him is to structure religious experience as if it were a pre-cut set of pieces to be assembled by following the instructions in the box. This is not to say that one may believe anything and call it faith in God. It is to say that we can neither impose our form of faith upon another nor simply adopt another's form for ourselves and hope to have any reality in it.

Some people experience God only in deep crisis, others out of a life of quiet regularity. Some experience faith in God with a great burst of emotion; others, as did Lewis, through a rational process. Some are overwhelmed, as Saul of Tarsus. Some cannot recall a time when they did not believe.

IV

Coping

1

When the House Is On Fire

On election day when I was six our house burned. My grandfather had been to vote. We were sitting at the dinner table, being served by my grandmother who was in a wheelchair, when neighbors burst in to announce that flames and smoke were billowing out of the upstairs windows.

Grandpa ran to the door which enclosed the stairway of the frame house he had built himself, tore open the door, and as quickly slammed it when he saw the fire eating its way down the stairs. They herded us grandchildren out into the yard with my grandmother, who when somebody yelled "Fire!" had run out of the house and left her wheelchair to burn up.

With the woman and children safely out, the men began to carry things out into the yard before the roof caved in. What a motley assortment of odds and ends they saved! An old iron cookstove that must have weighed half a ton, a few beat-up chairs and a bureau, a mattress, and bedsprings. That was about all. We didn't have many valuables in that Oklahoma farmhouse, but such as the family possessed went up in flames along with the house.

People do strange things when the house is on fire. They panic and lose perspective. This appears to be true of a culture, too, in an era of crisis.

When the house is on fire some stand around and intone, "The house is on fire, the house is on fire," as if the announcement would put it out. Some pitch in and lend a hand, but we always seem to have more heralds of the conflagration than helpers to fight it or save the valuables from it. Unfortunately, some who do come to help are as compulsive and unreflective as my grandpa and his neighbors in choosing what to save from the fire. And a lot of people just take off and run.

No unusual perceptiveness is needed to see that the house of our culture is on fire. It is not just Watergate that made this evident, but the cynicism about the American political process which made it possible. It is not simply that the American people lost confidence in the integrity of the executive branch of government, but that they suspect that many who feign outrage are not so admirable themselves. Are Watergate and Chappaquiddick to be this generation's bequest to the American dream? Is this the best that our age can produce?

It is not simply that the American balance of payments is so unfavorable to the dollar that it is no longer respected abroad, but that nobody appears to know how to salvage it. The problem is not simply that inflation is destroying the security of millions of Americans on fixed incomes, but that both big business and big labor show little evidence of concern.

It is not simply that the individual citizen feels powerless, but that he feels no inspiration. It is not only that there is a general uneasiness about the moral condition of the country, but that few of us are willing to look in the mirror and say, "You are the man!"

Hand-wringing lamentation is tempting, but unproductive. Flight into some kind of safe retreat is also hard to resist but not very helpful. Multitudes are doing one or the other— lamenting or running, or both.

People who are taking flight into alcohol or other drugs are running. People who are retreating to their hideaways at the lake or beach or in the mountains, or taking extensive and frequent trips abroad are probably running. People who spend all day over bridge or at parties are probably running from our problems. People who have escaped into some form of otherworldly religion which encourages preoccupation with spirituality to the exclusion of participation in the social and moral concerns of the day are taking flight.

Withdrawal is most attractive. When life becomes so confusing as to offer only unthinkable options, escape seems necessary. It is the most common mood of the college campus. In the sixties the mood was one of angry confrontation. Students made demands. Today they just want to be let alone.

But running away when the house is on fire is no more constructive than standing around making the announcement. Somebody needs to get busy and organize the help available to put the fire out, or at least salvage the valuables from it. How can that be done?

Let it begin with us—you and me. Let relationships between us at home and at work take on a greater measure of integrity. Let us seek to hear what each other is saying and ask ourselves more searching questions about the moral directions of our families, our churches, our businesses.

Let us examine our own priorities in the light of the nation's welfare. Can no one inspire us to put the welfare of the country above our personal gain and private enjoyment? Have we as a people lost the capacity for moral indignation and unselfish decision?

The word from God's Word is that we humans do not learn much from experience. We tend to make the same mistakes again and again. But the word is not one of despair; it is a word of hope, for God has the last word. He makes even the wrath of man to praise him.

2

The Alligators and the Swamp

My friend the physician sent me the following aphorism: "It is the duty of every administrator to anticipate problems, not simply to react to them, and by far-sighted, efficient, fair, logical and constructive planning prevent troubles long before they arise. However, it is sometimes difficult to remember that your original mission was to drain the swamp when you are up to Poupart's ligament in alligators."

He knew I would need help with "Poupart's ligament," so he added a note explaining that it is located at the junction of the thigh and abdomen at the groin. Now the aphorism makes sense to us ordinary folks. But can you think about draining the swamp when you are up to your hips in alligators?

I suppose that nearly every problem confronting this country is compounded by the swamp-alligator dilemma. Do you attack the causes of inflation, unemployment, crime, decaying cities, and all the rest, or do you try to deal with the consequences—the alligators?

I am especially concerned about the specter of mass starvation, chronic malnutrition, and hunger of a billion human beings on the globe. I have urged people to inform themselves, get involved, find a reliable relief organization and give significantly, and most of all, reexamine their personal priorities and urge our government to give leadership in the restructuring of national priorities.

But I am continually reminded—by myself as well as others—that such actions, well-intentioned as they are, do not drain the swamp but only fight off the alligators. One man sent me an illuminating and persuasive paper concerning the necessity to limit population growth. Across the top of the first page he had written, "Tonight there will be 225,000 more people for dinner."

He wants to drain the swamp. We have to limit the growth of the alligators before they devour everything in sight. I couldn't agree more, but I am not at all sure that this can be done apart from some form of coercion or else by dramatically raising the standards of living of the overpopulated, underdeveloped countries. The first option is undesirable, while the second seems unlikely. In the meantime, the annual rate of population increase in undeveloped countries is three times that of developed countries.

The problem is further complicated by acts of medical mercy which save babies from dying and enable old people to live longer. The population burgeons, not because there are so many more births, but because more being born are living, and living longer.

"Are we really helping these people?" someone asks me. "Maybe we are interfering with nature's method of correcting man-made errors." Too many people means a lot of them have to starve so that things are brought into balance.

Because I am a Christian I am unable to accept that solution. That solution to world hunger denies Christ. Everything about him contradicts it. Whatever others may do, I have to care. Christ compels me. I cannot ignore my brother while his child starves.

So, since I cannot drain the swamp I suppose I shall busy myself contending with the alligators. I can keep two children alive with what I fritter away buying trinkets I don't need. Millions of Americans could each feed a child with the coins they idly drop into vending machines. I see students feeding quarters to pinball machines every day, and wish they cared as much for hungry children as they care for the flashing lights and ringing bells.

You see, to argue that you can't do anything about the alligators until somebody figures a way to drain the swamp is a cop-out. We can quote statistics about annual rainfall, changing climatic conditions, fertilizer needs, new strains of seed, optimal numbers of people, and all kinds of learned inquiries. All of that is important, and somebody needs to be working at those problems. But in the meantime, have you denied yourself a single thing so that somebody's child might eat today?

You say you don't know where to give the money to a reliable agency, that you don't want to be ripped off by an emotional appeal when half of what you give goes to support some plush agency in New York? I don't intend to be ripped off either, if I can help it. I hate being suckered.

But ask your minister, priest, or rabbi. He can tell you about a trustworthy, conscientious agency which is really feeding people and, better still, helping them to feed themselves. Most of the churches have a hunger relief program and persons on the spot where hunger exists.

3

To One Whose Loss Is Great

My friend is crushed by the dissolution of a valued ten-year relationship. "Like the trapped animal who gnaws off the caught limb, I have at horrible cost removed my physical existence from my home.

"The entire situation...resembles a nightmare of monumental proportions. Unbelief and agony are my constant companions. I've no home, no job worth anything, and have lost the one thing in the world I wanted more than my own life.... Now there's absolutely nothing left to salvage.... I have only a bucket of ashes that all my tears will never wash away.

"It doesn't seem to me that it should be possible for one person to hurt as much as I do now. I rage ... at God who leads M. to believe one thing and me another. What sinister irony. Why, why, why? There is no comfort to be had anywhere. I feel so beaten down, broken, and so vastly alone."

What shall I say to my friend? Cheer up, it might be worse? Don't be so dramatic, it's not all that bad? Don't worry about it, someone else will come along to fill the emptiness?

If I were to write any of those glib things, I would deserve to lose a friend, for I would have shown that I either do not care a great deal about my friend or else do not understand the nature of grief. Neither is true.

What can I say to one whose loss is so great? Maybe the only thing worth saying is, "I'm sorry you are hurt. I wish I could take part of the hurt into myself so that you did not have so much to bear. Let me stand beside you and weep with you and support you in your sorrow."

Let me reassure my friend that grief is not an evidence of infidelity to God or an indication of weakness. The Bible is not reticent about expressing sorrow. About the Messiah one prophet wrote, "He was ... a man of sorrows, and acquainted with grief," and "Surely he has borne our griefs/and carried our sorrows" (Isa. 53:3-4, RSV). Weeping is not inappropriate. Jesus wept more than once.

I also want to tell my friend that anger—even at God—is OK. If God is as compassionate and wise a Father as I think he is, he is quite able to handle our hostility without needing to "zap" us for being angry at him.

Parents put up with hostility from their children, knowing that it is an appropriate though undeserved response to something that has happened to their children. Can't God be counted upon to be as loving? I think so.

Dr. Elizabeth Kubler-Ross met a mother whose child had just died in the hospital. "You look as though you need to scream," Dr. Ross said.

"Do you have a screaming room in the hospital?" the mother answered. "I need to scream and rage and curse. I've just been sitting in the parking lot and cursing and screaming at God."

The wise doctor said: "Do it here. It's better to do it with somebody than out in a parking lot all alone." I think God would approve.

But when my friend is able to listen, I want to say that neither despondency nor anger is a healthy, long-range companion. We have to get beyond them before we can get well.

There is a fine point of difference between grief and self-pity. Grief over a real loss is appropriate. Self-pity is a poisonous drug that incapacitates and destroys. When I am tempted to feel sorry for myself I try to say to myself: "Hey, who promised you a rose garden? Life is the great gift. You have no claim on God. To live is a bonus. Why should you suppose that you have the right to live without pain and anxiety and disappointment?"

I have no idea why some people appear to have less trouble than others. Why was I born an American, reasonably intelligent, and given the personal drive to get an education and make something out of myself? I earned none of that, any more than I deserved some of the bad things that have happened to me.

So I say to my friend: "You are young, healthy, intelligent, well-educated, with parents and friends who care about you. Your life is far from over; it is only just begun. Not for a moment do I discount the intensity of your pain. But you must let go of it. Surrender it. Let it become a part of that cherished chamber of memory which both blesses and burns.

"You absolutely must not allow yourself to wallow. In time

that would destroy you as a person. The relationship you grieve for is over. That part of your life is done. Let it be.

"God can use the pain you are having to make of you a more beautiful and loving person. Grief's highest employment is in helping other grievers. I am sorry you are hurt. When you are ready, God will help you put the hurt to good use."

4

Learning to Cope with Loneliness

Never were there so many of us living on planet Earth, never were people in such close proximity, and never was there so much going on to keep us occupied and amused. And probably never have people felt more isolated and alone. Here is a problem that includes most of us. In the tender film, *The Heart Is a Lonely Hunter,* Mick, a beautiful teenage girl struggling with adolescence, says wonderingly to Mr. Singer, a sensitive deaf-mute, "You're lonely, too! And I thought I was the only one." Yes, Mick, everyone struggles with the fear of being isolated. However there are some valid antidotes, not gimmicks or tricks, but ways people learn to cope.

One is working on the development of a self that you can respect. This involves, first, clarifying who you are, as distinguished from parents, brothers and sisters, classmates, mate, fellow employees, or anybody else. It involves developing reasonable expectations of yourself, not simply accepting expectations imposed upon you, although you give weight to others' understanding of your potential and limitations.

Self-respect comes also from the cultivation of what you find fulfilling and meaningful. Many a man dribbles his life away in things that have no meaning for him. Little wonder he feels useless.

It means remaining open and capable of change and growth. As you get older the surest way to be miserable is to batten down all the hatches of your life so as to protect yourself from the swirling winds of challenge and change. People who don't nail down the doors and windows may take a beating from the storm, but they sure don't dry up and wither away from boredom.

If a self you can respect is the first clue to coping with loneliness, finding significant others to care for is the second. This does not mean latching onto people who can "do something for you" or whom you can smother with neurotic need to be a "fixer," playing God with other people's lives. It does mean significant relationships in which something more than surface sensations is happening between the people involved.

Significant relations with others require time, honest concern, and the surrender of freedom to control one's situation. People who will have friends only on their own terms or only when they need them do not have any friends. They may have relationships based upon some form of functional dependency, either their dependency on the other or the other's on them. But this kind of "I will call when I need you" relationship is not friendship.

The popular song, "People Who Need People Are the Luckiest People in the World," is psychologically unsound on two counts. It suggests that there are people who don't need people. People who don't need people aren't people. You are a person at all only because other persons have always been around to meet your needs. Even before you came into the world you lived off another person, and you have been feeding on the sustenance given by others ever since.

More than that, there is a lot of neurotic feeling in the song,

"People Who Need People." If you concentrate on needing people you may not be a very good candidate for significant relationships. It would be a better song if it went, "People who know that they are needed by people." But that one probably would not sell many records—it's too healthily honest.

Loneliness is not the same as being alone. You don't have to have somebody chattering in your ear constantly or holding your hand. Mere bodily presence with another may be a lonely experience, as many a person can testify. On the contrary, one may live alone and feel greatly supported by his kinship with his fellowmen.

5

Hardship Can Produce Unexpected Dividends

You don't always get what you think is coming to you, and often that is a blessing. Many a life-transaction produces unexpected dividends which, while not necessarily superior to those hoped for, have a quality all their own. For a clear example read the letters of the apostle Paul. One of the most moving and revealing is Philippians, named for the people to whom he wrote it. Paul was in jail awaiting a trial that might conclude with a death sentence. Friends had sent to inquire after him, and the letter is his response to their concern.

He was getting along quite well, he said, continually cheered by recollection of their friendship. He was unsure of the outcome of the trial, but certain it would turn out to God's glory, and he wished them not to be unduly alarmed for him. The prospects for his release were less important than the possible effects of his imprisonment on the Cause.

From our perspective, it is unfortunate that Paul was not concerned enough about his own welfare to discuss it more fully. But it is a testimony to the greatness of the man. It was not flippancy that kept him from saying more, but preoccupation with the unexpected dividends which the inconveniences and hardships of his imprisonment had produced.

He does not say, "Don't worry about me; all is for the best." He does say that certain good things have happened that might never have come about except for his imprisonment. Read how he put it: "I want you to know, brethren, that what has happened to me has really served to advance the gospel" (Phil. 1:12, RSV).

Three unexpected dividends were cited: (1) It had become known throughout the praetorian guard and among all the rest of the military establishment that his imprisonment was for Christ. Public interest had been aroused and questions were being asked about his religion. The prisoner obviously was no common criminal. Why was he in jail? Oh, for his faith? Well. Rather than hindering the spread of the gospel, putting Paul in prison had spread it.

(2) "Most of the brethren have been made confident ... because of my imprisonment" (Phil. 1:14, RSV), he wrote. The church had been stirred to new zeal and effort. His going to jail had affected those inside the Christian faith as well as impressing those outside it. His bonds gave others greater courage.

Of course, the missionary continued, not all fellow Christians admired him. Some were glad he was in jail because they opposed his kind of preaching. Perhaps they saw the occasion as an opportunity to advance their own brand of Christianity. Very well, at least the word of Christ was being spoken, even if in controversy.

(3) The other unexpected dividend was that loyal friends such as the Philippians had been stirred to a new concern to

pray for the ministry of the missionary. "I know that through your prayers and the help of the Spirit of Jesus Christ this will turn out for my deliverance" (Phil. 1:19, KJV), Paul said.

He was not saying that he was confident that he was going to be cleared of the charges against him when his case came to trial. Rather, he was saying that their prayers and the sustaining of the Spirit of Christ would enable him to be delivered from the temptation to surrender to fear. With full courage he would honor Christ with his body, whether by life or by death, and give the good witness. With such full commitment he would be delivered from the bondage of excessive self-concern.

Is it not often the case that things have a way of turning out, not just differently but better than we thought they would? Here is the way Emerson put it in a celebrated essay: "As no man had ever a point of pride that was not injurious to him, so no man ever had a defeat that was not somewhere made useful to him." That is not automatically so, but if we make unselfish investment there are always unexpected dividends.

6

The Pain God Is Allowed to Guide

I know a little about pain—everybody does—but I am not an expert in its management. I have tried to go to school to courageous, victorious people who can teach me the good uses of pain, but I still have a lot to learn.

Philosophizing about pain comes easy for me. I give lectures on the subject. What if the world were made without the possibility of our suffering or inflicting pain? I ask. What if the ground yielded so that I did not bruise when I fall on my face? What if I felt nothing when I put my hand in the fire?

What if God restricted my choices to those which would result only in my well-being and the well-being of everybody whom my choices affect? Moreover, if God makes it possible for me to care for other people, am I not vulnerable to pain when they experience pain? God would have had to give me the mind of an oyster if he intended to protect me from pain.

Then does that mean that God is responsible for my pain? Yes, in the sense that even he could not make me with the capabilities of being human without being vulnerable.

But that is not the same thing as saying that God inflicts pain upon us. Often we do that to ourselves. If we play Russian roulette we must not blame God if the gun goes off. God gets blamed for a lot of malice, greed, and stupidity.

Sometimes pain is the result of another's sin or folly. Our lives are so interrelated that we cannot limit consequences of our behavior, good or evil, to ourselves. I often think of that when a student defiantly tells me that it's his life and he will blow his chances if he wants to. Not so. There are parents and grandparents and former generations and future generations—all of whom own a piece of him.

Sometimes pain comes from a mysterious and inexplicable set of circumstances over which neither the sufferer nor anyone else has control. Lightning strikes, a tornado shatters a home like a matchbox, an artery explodes, cancer claims another victim.

No situation involving persons is wholly without a human factor, someone argues. Perhaps so, but multitudes of occasions defy the easy explanation that "if So-and-so had not done such-and-such this would not have happened." There is enough unexplained pain on any street to make one wonder.

As much as I enjoy hearing myself lecture, I confess that I am quickly bored with philosophizing—especially if I am hurting. Nothing gets old quicker than moralizing about suffering when you are the sufferer.

We don't need explanations of our pain. We need help not to waste it when we have to endure it. If pain is unavoidable, are there positive uses of it, or is it a barren wasteland without beauty or meaning?

Paul, Christ's apostle to so many of us, wrote a helpful word about the use of pain: "The pain God is allowed to guide ends in a saving repentance never to be regretted, whereas the world's pain ends in death" (2 Cor. 7:10). Some people simply waste their pain. They learn nothing from it. It is a total loss.

But it need not be. Suppose God guides your pain? Suppose you surrender it to him and ask him what you can learn from what you have to suffer? "I have learned more from three prolonged illnesses than I have ever been able to get from books," wrote a prominent minister the last year of his life.

What do you imagine he learned from his pain? Maybe he learned how to listen to the cries of other people when they were in physical or psychic pain. If so, that was a great lesson.

Perhaps his pain brought him into what Albert Schweitzer used to call "the fellowship of those who bear the mark of pain." Here is what Schweitzer wrote: "Those who have learned by experience what physical pain and bodily anguish mean belong together all the world over; they are united by a secret bond." If you bear the mark of pain look closely into the eyes of the next person you meet, for you will probably see there a brother or sister.

Maybe the minister's three bouts with pain gave him greater ability to help others frightened by having to get acquainted with grief or pain. Suppose his pain made him what Father Henri J. Nouwen has called *The Wounded Healer?* Then he hadn't wasted his own pain.

Most important of all, the pain God is allowed to guide ends in a saving repentance never to be regretted. This is to say, pain surrendered to God enables us to change our minds, revise our priorities, and get things straight. Whether it is because of stubbornness or carelessness, we don't think too much about life's preciousness until it is threatened by pain.

We may forever regret having had to suffer the pain, but if God has helped us to put it to good use, we can celebrate. Even pain, if God is allowed to guide it, can bless us.

7

When You Don't Get First Choice

More than forty-five years ago now, Dr. Harry Emerson Fosdick preached a sermon that affected my life. I did not hear the sermon at the time, for I was an Oklahoma farm boy who had never heard of Harry Emerson Fosdick.

When I did hear about him it wasn't good. I was told he was a dangerous New York liberal who corrupted people with false religion. Perhaps curiosity impelled me to find out for myself. In any event, when I came across Fosdick's *Handling Life's Second-Bests* I knew it was not only true but important.

Life does not always give us our first choice, Dr. Fosdick said. Forced to take second or third best, we may so respond to what we didn't want but had to accept that we make it into something good and beautiful. That, he said, is the secret of nearly every unusual achievement. His argument was persuasive, evidence convincing.

There is that notable occasion in Paul's missionary travels when he wanted to go into the region of Bithynia, one of the richest provinces of Asia Minor, but was forbidden by the Spirit of Jesus. In a vision Paul saw a man who said, "Come over into Macedonia, and help us" (Acts 16:9, KJV). Paul wanted Bithynia, but Macedonia and Greece were thrust upon him. Here the gospel passed over from Asia into Europe—a momentous event for the future of Christianity, and for us. But Macedonia was not Paul's first choice.

Knowing Paul, one might reasonably assume that the decision to work in Bithynia had not been made casually. He never did anything tentatively. Being deprived of working in Bithynia must have been a disappointment, but think about how much came of Paul's doing his best with his second choice! Churches were established at Philippi, Thessalonica, and Corinth. And the ages received his epistles to the Philippians, Thessalonians, and Corinthians.

Was Paul unique in this experience? No, said the preacher, he is by no means an exception. Whistler, the artist, intended to have a military career but couldn't pass chemistry at West Point. "If silicon had been a gas," he used to say, "I should have been a major general." Failing in his first choice, Whistler halfheartedly tried engineering, then took up painting—with remarkable results.

Sir Walter Scott wanted to be a poet, but Lord Byron's work was so much more popular that Scott gave up poetry and turned to fiction. At first he published his stories anonymously, so timid was he about their merit. But the English-speaking world is lastingly indebted to him for accepting his Macedonia when the door to his Bithynia was closed.

Phillips Brooks wanted to be a teacher and plunged into the profession with enthusiasm after graduating from college. But he failed so miserably that he was discharged from his position, and wrote in despair: "I don't know what will become of me and I don't care much." But then he entered the ministry and became one of the stellar figures in the history of the American pulpit.

Consider Adoniram Judson, a modern counterpart of the missionary Paul. Judson's life was pledged to evangelizing India, but the East India Company would not let him stay there. For a whole year he tried in vain to gain admission, then turned, humiliated and disappointed, to Burma. There he handled his opportunity so admirably that his name will be revered so long as Christian missions is respected.

These were some of the examples Fosdick cited to show that people who don't get to do what they prefer need not be failures. But it was only after reading Fosdick's autobiography that I realized where his sermon came from. It came out of his personal experience, where all really powerful sermons originate.

When he was a second-year seminarian, Harry Emerson Fosdick had a complete nervous breakdown. He intended to become a professor, but his collapse and the necessity to get down to his own spiritual roots changed that. He knew after he got well that he was meant to be a preacher, not a professor.

In his mental depression, Fosdick said, he learned some things about religion that theological seminaries do not teach. "I learned to pray, not because I had adequately argued out prayer's rationality, but because I desperately needed help from a Power greater than my own. I learned that God, much more than a theological proposition, is an immediately available Resource."

V
No Place to Run

1

Courage to Fail

"Show me a good loser and I'll show you a loser," growled one of baseball's most colorful managers. "I do not think winning is the most important thing," said another, "I think winning is the only thing."

Maybe. "Winning-is-everything" seems to be the national creed. The unforgivable sin is to fail. From Little League to the World Series, from Soapbox Derby to the Indy 500, from Friday night high school football to the Superbowl, the name of the game is win. It would be hard to make a living in this country selling manuals on how to be a graceful loser!

Of course, losing has no inherent virtue. Failure carries no automatic benefit nor grace. Leo Durocher to the contrary, good guys don't always finish last, and finishing last is no guarantee of a sweet spirit. It may only indicate that you really are a loser. Some of the meanest people you will ever see are consistent losers.

Some people fail habitually because they don't care enough

to succeed. Lacking commitment to excellence, content with mediocrity, whether in work or play, they go unfeelingly from one shoddy performance to the next.

Others fail because they are afraid of failure. That sounds contradictory, but we can want so badly to succeed that we are not free to do our best. Some people get the name of "never being able to win the big one." Their problem is not lack of desire but excessive desire—fear of losing to the competition.

Still others fail because they program themselves to fail. They build failure into their plan, sometimes unconsciously, sometimes even consciously. "I'm not expected to do well," they tell themselves, so naturally they fulfill their own expectations.

Sometimes parents condition their children to a lifetime of failure. How many times does a child have to hear from his father or mother, "You can't do anything right, you always mess up," before he decides that he is just a born loser?

A student I see has the problem of self-defeat. He regularly programs himself to fail. He feels terribly guilty about wasting his parents' money, but he continues to behave in ways that guarantee he will fail as a student. Why won't he allow himself to succeed? Well, failure has become a way of life. He knows how to fail. He is an expert at it. What he and I are trying to do is to devise a way for him to learn how to succeed.

Despite all the negative things I have written about failure, I think that it has merit. I deplore the American myth that failure is the ultimate disgrace. That is obvious nonsense, for if it is possible to win it is also possible not to win. And if there is something to be won, then there is something to be lost. And if someone must win, someone must lose. Must it always be the other person, or may I not sometimes be "it" without incurring loss of face?

In John W. Gardner's thoughtful book, *Self-Renewal,* he writes about the need to risk failure in order to achieve: "One of the reasons why mature people are apt to learn less than young people is that they are willing to risk less. Learning is a risky business, and they do not like failure."

Watch the infant, Gardner argues, if you want to see a lesson in learning by failing. The child is learning at a phenomenal rate, and he is also experiencing a shattering number of failures. "See the innumerable things he tries and fails. And see how little the failures discourage him."

"With each year that passes," Gardner continues, "he will be less blithe about failure. . . . By middle age most of us carry in our heads a tremendous catalogue of things we have no intention of trying again because we tried them once and failed—or tried them once and did less well than our self-esteem demanded.

"We pay a heavy price for our fear of failure. It is a powerful obstacle to growth," Gardner writes. "If you want to keep on learning, you must keep on risking failure—all your life."

We do not grow to our full potential by endlessly repeating the easy feats learned when we were still hopeful and flexible enough to risk defeat. Only in the context of the real possibility of failure is there any real potential for the exhilaration of success.

2

When to Be Afraid

"Education consists in being afraid at the right time," a famous pundit once commented. Excusing oversimplification, the description merits thoughtful consideration. Joseph Fort

Newton at the end of a long ministry wrote in his autobiography, *River of Years,* that fear is man's number one nemesis. He said that if he could preach only one sermon it would be about how to manage fear.

Of course, fear is not a total liability. It is often useful, even essential. The human race would not have survived without this built-in alarm system sensitively keyed to spur the organism to fight or flight at sign of danger.

The late Harry Emerson Fosdick loved to spend his summers on the Maine coast. Once he said that only landlubbers, visiting on the coast, were not afraid of the ocean. They had no idea what the tide can do, or what a heavy sea can mean, or what being lost in a fog without a compass is like, or the great difference it makes to miss the channel by a mere ten feet. The experienced have a healthy awe of the sea.

Indeed, fear can be a powerfully creative motive. Schools are in part the result of fear of ignorance. Industry owes its existence to the fear of poverty and want. The advances of medical science grow out of fear of disease. And many a man has sought the supportive comfort of God because he was afraid.

I used to think it was bad to excite fear in order to cause people to think about their eternal destiny. One day an old minister said, "The trouble with you young preachers is that you don't know much about human nature. A lot of things may turn a man to repentance and faith. Your trouble is that if you can't get a man to respond from the highest motive—love— you don't ask him to respond at all. Maybe his spiritual condition is such that he can't answer the appeal of love. You must be willing to reach him where he is—in the realm of fear. After that he may learn to love."

It was a valid rebuke. Sometimes we have to have the "fear of God" put in us before we are willing to do what we should have done on the basis of love. That is why fear may be a redemptive force in personal life and in the social order.

But fear may also be destructive. It is so when it runs riot, goes out of bounds. For clarity, call such uncontrolled and unreasonable fear anxiety. It is fear that is obsessive, abnormal, disproportionate to the situation. Like fire, a great and valuable servant but ruinous and fearsome force when out of control, is fear when it has become anxiety.

A wise parent teaches a child to be careful in crossing the street, but suppose the parent instills in the child such anxiety about street-crossing that he freezes into immobility whenever he steps from a curb? It is good to teach a child to be wary of strangers, but suppose you make her so terrified of new situations that she cannot go to school without such great anxiety that she frequently becomes physically ill. Fear, given as a tool, has become in such cases a dreadful weapon. Most often it is a weapon turned upon oneself for mutilation or destruction.

How does fear get out of hand? Sometimes it does because of ignorance. We are afraid of what we cannot understand. Clifford Beers provides a tragic illustration of this from his own life. In his book, *The Mind That Found Itself,* he records his bitter experience of years in and out of insanity. He had an epileptic brother, thought the condition was contagious, and lived on the edge of fear until he finally went over it into insanity.

Sometimes excessive fear is the product of hostility and guilt. It is terribly important to our mental health to sense a "rightness" in relationships. When things are not right—between us and others—anxiety is an almost inevitable product of the disruption.

Much that Jesus said to his followers has to do with the destructive power of unwarranted fear. He kept calling people out of themselves, away from preoccupation with their anxieties, and tried to attach them in faith to God and to their fellowmen. Such trust in God and service to one's fellows is the best antidote for abnormal fear.

3

Staying Is Harder Than Getting There

At a dinner party a friend said, "In my time I must have lost several hundred pounds." Losing weight is no problem. Keeping it off is the trick.

Staying is harder than getting there. A physician's study showed that fifty percent of patients who had reduced their weight had regained it all during two or three years, and ninety percent had gained it all back after nine years.

A writer told of deciding to exercise regularly to improve his health. So he began jogging in the early morning and found it a pleasant and rewarding way to lose weight. He also felt better and had more energy. Friends and family rewarded him with remarks about his improved appearance, and he experienced a lot of satisfaction in the achievement of his goals.

However, lovely summer mornings gave way to dark, cold, wet days of fall and winter, and he realized that it was going to be much harder to stay fit and trim than it had been getting that way. "If I were to keep what I had gained, there lay before me the prospects of doing calisthenics and running, day in and day out, in good weather and in bad, for the rest of my life."

In almost anything we undertake staying is harder than getting there. Most of us can generate enough enthusiasm and energy to make a good start, or a good impression, or begin a good relationship. It's keeping going that is hard. We run out of steam. When the novelty wears off we have to have a new challenge—a new job, a new town, a new partner. Weight control, then, is not so much a special kind of problem as it is part of the whole business of living. The issue is whether we can keep long-term commitments.

The Bible reflects concern for this common human difficulty. Jesus told about a man who began to build a tower but ran out of materials before it was finished, and had to leave it standing there as an ugly monument to his shortsightedness. Jesus also told about a king who began a war but gave up the battle because he had not first adequately inventoried his resources.

Paul put the matter succinctly in his epistle to the Galatians. As the *Good News Bible* translates it, Paul says: "So let us not become tired of doing good; for if we do not give up, the time will come when we will reap the harvest" (6:9). We fail for many reasons, but probably most often because we just get tired.

Excitement will see us through a football game. Sentimentalism and romanticism will give us incentive to do temporary and occasional acts of "rescuing the down-and-out." Bravery may enable us to run into a burning house to save a child. But the lifelong work of living for others requires more than a shot of spiritual adrenaline.

What keeps us staying there when we have gotten there? Careful attention to the "contract," for one thing. What exactly are we agreeing to do? The worst thing that can happen to our sense of commitment is to get into something and then find that we promised more than we intended, that the expectations were different from our understanding of them.

It also helps to focus upon the part of the task that is at hand, rather than trying to keep it all in view all the time. If I permit myself to become preoccupied with everything I have to do this month, I shall never get done what I need to do today. Step-by-step, we must meet life. Jesus said, "So do not worry about tomorrow; it will have enough worries of its own. There is no need to add to the troubles each day brings" (Matt. 6:34, TEV).

A third step for staying committed is to reevaluate and renegotiate the contract from time to time. Maybe we are doing something resentfully and halfheartedly, or perhaps we have defaulted upon a promise and don't know what to do about failure and guilt. Take another look at the contract with the person with whom it was made. Maybe anger and hostility are needless. Perhaps the need has changed and the contract also needs to be brought up-to-date.

4

Without Courage We Perish

Alexander Solzhenitsyn, using Harvard's commencement for a platform, said Americans are gutless wonders without moral courage to survive in a world full of danger. Mrs. Rosalynn Carter, lately of Plains, Georgia, says it's not so. One must hope that she is right and the Nobel Prize winner wrong about us, for, if not, we are in bad trouble. However, we cannot lightly dismiss Solzhenitsyn's comment. People who scorn prophets too often fulfill their prophecies.

I don't know whether the exiled Russian novelist is a prophet or an ingrate, but I do believe that a nation mainly concerned for its pleasure and comfort is sowing the seeds of its own ruin. Historians such as Gibbons and Toynbee argued that the Romans got tired of being courageous and wanted mainly to be entertained.

Would less self-indulgence have made any difference in the outcome? Were the Vandals and Goths going to overrun the place, no matter what the Romans did? Was the Roman Empire a victim of historical necessity? Did its rise and fall illustrate the hymn which says, "Our little systems have their day, they have their day and cease to be"? Some think so. We, too, may be helpless victims of a process that works with inexorable certainty. If so, forget about courage. We may as well eat, drink, and be merry, for tomorrow we die—or more likely, the day after tomorrow our children do.

On the other hand, if we believe that individual and corporate behavior makes a difference in a people's destiny, we must think about courage. Courage, perhaps more than native ability or environmental advantage, affects our response to adversity. Courage is a quality of heart, the word being derived from the Latin word meaning heart. Courage is mostly identified with heroism in battle, or fortitude in pain or danger. But moral courage is harder than physical bravery.

Thomas Aquinas spoke of courage as "strength of mind, capable of conquering whatever threatens attainment of the highest good." Moral courage is not inherited, nor produced by something you drink, nor the result of giving or receiving pep talks. We may whip up enthusiasm to "fight hard" in a ball game, but that is not moral courage.

Courage is an act of the will through which one decides not to seek one's safety or pleasure or comfort first, but to behave in ways congruent with what one conceives to be the highest good. Self-denial, self-discipline, or unusual effort all require moral courage.

Sometimes great moral courage is required simply to cope with the awesome mystery of life itself. It is the kind of fortitude Paul Tillich termed *The Courage to Be.* There are times when about the best one can do is to call out, as did Hopeful in Bunyan's *Pilgrim's Progress,* "Be of good cheer, my brother!"

Moral courage is required to deal with change. Our lives are in process. Few things will stand still for us to enjoy them endlessly. Nothing is really fixed. The sun may have stood still for Joshua once, but it keeps moving for us. I can't control the changes that are coming about in me, but I can control my response to them. That is where courage helps.

Moral courage is required to respond adequately to failure. Nobody's life is an unbroken string of wins, no losses. To be able to accept defeat when it is not your fault, to forgive yourself and try again when it is your fault, and to go on living creatively in any circumstance, requires courage.

Moral courage is needed to resist appeals to live a shabby, grubby, and hedonistic existence. In magazine, newspaper, and on TV, that kind of self-destructive behavior is too frequently honored and held out as enviable. Daily we make decisions whether to copy such antics or to live a godly life.

Whether Solzhenitsyn or Rosalynn Carter is right about us, history will tell. But unless we have decided that our own personal behavior makes no difference, we can think and act with moral courage. Without courage we cannot survive as a people.

5

No Place to Run

A feature about middle-aged executives and bored housewives who "cut and run" in our high-pressure society caught my eye as I thumbed through a national news weekly. Since no law exists against deserting society, nobody knows just how many adults run away from their responsibilities and families each year, but estimates run in the hundreds of thousands.

The profile of the average adult male runaway shows a successful professional or business executive forty-four to fifty-one years of age, college-educated, making about $25,000 a year with a liberal expense account, bored and discontented with what he considers the phoniness of his world, and most of all, pressured. A bigger house, bigger car, country club, with all the extra payments to be made, have pushed him to the brink.

He may turn to alcohol or drugs, or have a nervous breakdown. A few commit suicide. But increasing numbers are simply dropping out. Some morning John Doe, a successful suburbanite, kisses his wife, pats the dog, gives the children their allowances, gets in his car for the office just as on any other work day. Only this time he never goes to work.

Likely his distraught family will track him down. He may be found living in a flophouse in a great city, seeking anonymity and irresponsibility. He may be discovered working at a manual labor job or pursuing an old hobby. He may agree to come back, and he may not.

About as many women as men run away. The woman runaway is younger—about thirty-five. She married early, had children right away, and after fifteen years of nesting, is bored and unfulfilled. Her attempts to help her husband and children are interpreted by them as nagging and meddling. She feels unappreciated, stifled, and locked into a dull job—chief cook and bottle washer—with little opportunity to use her education and her mind.

Male or female, runaways are looking for a simpler, more peaceful, more satisfying, and authentic life. Most of all, they feel they are in an intolerable situation. Does the runaway find the life for which he longs? Sometimes, but usually not. There is no end of the rainbow, much less a pot of gold. He or she may exchange pressures, but not be free of pressure. Sooner or later, we discover that we have used up our running room.

What do we do then? The mature person, I'm convinced, makes a stand. He finds a way to readjust the demands and pressures so that they are manageable. He rearranges his priorities in order to bring order out of the chaos about him.

The Bible is a storehouse of guidance about the urge to cut and run. Nehemiah, commissioned to rebuild the walls of Jerusalem after they had laid in ruins for seventy-five years, soon encountered staggering opposition. Some viewed the project as a threat to their own security. They warned of dire consequences if Nehemiah kept on with the work.

Some introduced division among his workers. Others started false rumors that Nehemiah was ripping-off the treasury for personal gain. Some said Nehemiah really wanted to be a king and planned to use the rebuilt wall as a fortress.

Things got so bad that someone came and urged him to give up, and take refuge on the horns of the altar in the Temple. At this point Nehemiah said a fine thing: "Should such a man as I run away?" Then he gave an unequivocal answer: "I will not run" (Neh. 6:11). I suspect Nehemiah did not run because he knew he couldn't live with himself if he gave in to pressure.

It is unrealistic for some people to assume Nehemiah's courage, because the pressure becomes truly unbearable when they are trying to bear it alone. Nehemiah had a resource available to us all, but not used by all. He believed that the Lord wanted that wall built and that the Lord wanted *him* to build it. Nehemiah accepted that task as a commitment. Therefore, he could take courage in the belief that he was doing God's work, no matter what his opponents said or did.

People who have those kinds of commitments and convictions, who have those kinds of promises to keep, find a way of bracing up when life gets hard. They may have to fall back and regroup, but it is unlikely they will run.

6

Knocked Down But Not Out

When he was old the Reverend John Watson, known among his fellow Scots as Ian Maclaren, declared that if he had his ministry to do over he would preach more comforting sermons. Asked why, he said: "Because most people are fighting a hard battle."

Watson lived in nineteenth-century Victorian Great Britain. The battle grows no easier in late twentieth-century America. Watch people's faces, look into pain-filled eyes, listen to the anguish in their voices, and you will know that many are fighting a hard battle.

My friends kid me about working in an ivory tower, the college campus. Students are presumed to have no problems more severe than being without a date for the spring prom. That may be the way you remember it, but it is not how I am experiencing it.

There is enough pain on any dormitory hall to make a marble statue weep. Broken homes, often broken as soon as the "kids are off to college," parental desertion, alcoholism, illness, or sudden death, are many a student's agenda. Such is the agenda of all persons sooner or later, and students are persons living through a crucial period of life when they are neither children nor mature adults. That is to say that they are especially vulnerable to being hurt.

What I see must be only the tip of the iceberg of pain. What any minister sees of the anguish of his people is only a fraction of the whole. Most people are fighting a hard battle indeed, and they likely do need more comforting sermons.

I try to remember that, but it is easier for me to scold. I find it easier to point out what is wrong than to celebrate what is right. I suspect that I am not unique, but I still must remind myself that we all need all the support we can get.

Rebuke and a call to repent are also needed, of course. Prophets are most often found summoning people to repentance. But they also need to hear the Lord's word to the prophet Isaiah: "Comfort ye, comfort ye my people" (Isa. 40:1, KJV).

Paul's experience in the first century may instruct us as to how we can respond when life threatens to overwhelm us. In a letter written to friends in Corinth he alludes to a dangerous crisis through which he has come by God's grace.

The apostle never tells what nearly did him in, but its severity is certain. Several times he was nearly lynched by a hostile mob, and the situation referred to in the letter to Corinth may well have been one of those occasions. He was "so utterly, unbearably crushed that [he] despaired of life itself." He felt that he "had received the sentence of death."

With God's help he survived. "He delivered us from so deadly a peril," Paul wrote, "and he will deliver us; on him we have set our hope that he will deliver us again" (2 Cor. 1:8-10, RSV). God had not just rescued him once; he was doing it again and again. God continued to bail him out when he could not bail himself out.

In a series of four figures taken from the battlefield Paul describes his continuing struggle to survive. "We are afflicted in every way, but not crushed." "Afflict" meant to press or squeeze. It was what happened to a hapless person crushed by a mob. *The New English Bible* reads: "Hard-pressed on every side, we are never hemmed in" (2 Cor. 4:8). The pressure was enormous, but God always provided a way out.

We are "perplexed, but not driven to despair" (2 Cor. 4:8, RSV). Here Paul used a play on words which is lost in translation. But the meaning remains. In the heat of battle he often did not know the solution to the problem at hand. But he was never driven to his wit's end. God always gave him the courage to go on even when he could not see the end of the road he was on.

We are "persecuted, but not forsaken" (2 Cor. 4:9, RSV). The enemy presses him and pursues him. But his Commander has not abandoned him to the foe. You can stand the pressure when you know that there are those who haven't abandoned you. Most of all, when you realize that God has not given up on you you can survive.

Finally, we are "struck down, but not destroyed" (Moffat). Charles Williams puts this line into fresh images: "We are always getting a knockdown, but never a knockout." What Paul seems to have been alluding to is the condition of the soldier felled by his opponent who is rescued by a friend just before the deathblow is struck by the enemy. He was not given the deathblow. He lived to fight another battle. God goes on saving him from these life-threatening encounters.

Thus he never gives up his hope. Life is tough, to be sure, but not hopeless. He has received a commission to engage in a cause greater than his own life. He is involved in something bigger than himself. With such credentials he cannot give in to hopelessness.

Moreover, he has experienced the excitement and reassurance of rescue. How could he ever surrender to despair when he has known the exhilaration of recovery from the brink of death?

All this has so changed his perspective and his personal goals that he has given up small ambitions and face-saving devices. He no longer sweats the small stuff. He is no longer primarily concerned with his own comfort or advancement, or even with survival. That is why he can write with such confidence that he can be knocked down, but not knocked out.

7

Responding to Challenge

A case can be made that character, personal or national, is the product of hard challenges more than of anything else. Not only character, but ingenuity, creativity, and achievement are all responses provoked by problems to be solved. Few geniuses have addresses on Easy Street.

Charles Kingsley, Victorian clergyman-novelist who advocated what his critics scorned as "muscular Christianity," wrote a little story called "The History of the Great and Famous Nation of the Doasyoulikes." They fled the country of Hardwork because they wanted to dance and play the harp all day. After a while they turned into gorillas.

Arnold Toynbee claimed that civilizations arose neither out of superior race nor favorable climate nor geography, but out of what he called "Challenge-and-Response." He wrote, "Neither race nor environment, taken by itself, can be the positive factor which, within the last six thousand years, has shaken humanity out of its static repose on the level of primitive society and started it on the hazardous quest of civilization."

If neither race nor environment produced civilization, what did? The stimulus of hard challenges, the historian replied. It was the stimulus of blows, of harshness, of pressures, of penalties, that incited peoples to greatness.

Why doesn't every community respond to challenge? Almost every challenge that has eventually evoked a victorious response has baffled or broken a hundred or a thousand others. What, at last, made the difference? Toynbee argued that it was an indefinable spiritual quality in the individuals, interacting upon their society and changing it. The "source of action" is in the individual. All growth originates with creative individuals or small minorities of individuals, who view their task as twofold: first, the achievement of their vision, whatever it may be; and second, the conversion of the society to this new way to life.

Now, if we require the "stimulus of harshness, blows, pressures, and penalties" in order to grow, then we need to take a fresh look at our attitudes toward adversity. This is not to suggest that one should court adversity. Such an approach to life would be pathological. It is to suggest that one need not resign oneself to enduring adversity, but may resolve to discover in adversity the hidden but real opportunity for growth.

The individual is the responding soul that challenges adversity. He generates that positive spark of challenge in himself, and then he lights another's fire, and that one another's. But you can't light any fires if your own has gone out.

VI

Is Marriage Obsolete?

1

Marriage Bonds—Not Bondage

What can be said to people who claim they want a stable, healthy marriage, but continue to behave toward one another in disruptive, even destructive, ways? Not everyone in a bad marriage wants help. Some just want out.

Frequently a marriage counselor finds himself used as an acceptable means of getting out. After a while the counselor gets the feeling that one or the other of the partners is merely going through the motions, wearing down, and waiting out the other partner, so that at the end of the abortive effort to save the marriage he may say self-righteously: "See, we tried counseling and it did no good. The marriage can't be salvaged. We can't live together; therefore I am justified in breaking it up."

How do you make a bad marriage better? First, you have to want to. People have to act on their desires to improve, rather than sit around hoping things will work out. That applies to marriage, as well as to any other personal relationship. When a couple comes for marriage counseling, the first thing I try to ascertain is the depth of commitment each has to the marriage. This is not to say that no situation is intolerable. It is to say that few, if any, are hopeless, if two people really want to make their marriage good.

An essential ingredient in a good marriage is self-respect on the part of each, and respect for one another. Though it sounds elementary, this is surprisingly hard for some people to practice. Freedom to be who you are, and permission for your partner to be who he or she is, marks a healthy relationship. You don't need to be the Bobbsey Twins.

Where there is the need to dominate and possess or to cling in parasitic dependence, you have a bad relationship. Healthy self-regard allows one to enjoy the other person for himself, not simply for his ability to satisfy one's needs. Self-regard also makes it possible for one to enjoy the sense of his own being over and above the value which his partner gives to him.

Dependency is bad medicine. If something happens to take away whatever we are dependent upon, we are literally wiped out. "I can't go on without him (her)" is the normal reaction. Then the dependent partner discovers that he not only must but can live without the other, and all kinds of resentment and acting out may follow. There is no bitterness like that of a person, deprived of his dependency, who has learned that he can do without it.

To make a good marriage, one must be willing to listen to one's partner, not just to words but to feelings. We often hear the other's words but do not hear what the other is telling us about ourselves or about himself, because we are too preoccupied with our own feelings. Thus we hear what we have "programmed" ourselves to hear, which may not be what the other intends at all. As the third party in a counseling situation, it is astonishing to me how marriage partners talk "past" one another. I sit and say to myself, "How could he miss what she is telling him? How could she not hear the message in what he is saying?"

Akin to developing the capacity to hear, and a complement

of it, is the art of telling the other what is happening to you. I very much like the use of "I" messages, a technique suggested in the "Parent Effectiveness Training" program for dealing with children. The "I" message is a way of letting the other person know how what he is doing is affecting you. Instead of passing judgment on the other, lambasting him for being bad, you try to help him see what is happening to you as a result of his behavior.

The person who gives an "I" message does not say, "How could you be so stupid, or thoughtless, or selfish or evil?" That almost certainly puts the other person on the defensive. Instead one says, "Your behavior makes me very sad, or insecure, or unloved or afraid." In short, the "I" message lets the other person know just where you are and what his behavior is doing to the relationship between you.

The other may respond by saying, "That's your problem. Tough." But if the other cares for you that person will more likely want to say, "How can I make you feel better? What can I do to help you get over this hurt?"

Marriage bonds need not become bondage.

2

Making a Marriage Better

Marriage is such a full-time, demanding association that a great many people in this society have trouble maintaining it. If you don't get along with a friend, you can walk away or drift apart, usually with a minimum of hurt. If you cannot work for your boss, you can usually find another job. Breaking up a home is something else—or should be, but a sick marriage may succumb without administration of such healing medicines as patience, kindness, trust, and trustworthiness.

Take patience, for example. People may need time and room to make necessary changes. Sometimes the most loving act one performs for his partner in a troubled relationship is to say—and mean—"I know it is hard for you to give up this person—habit—attitude—which is disrupting our relationship. I cannot expect you to act as if nothing has happened. Help me to be patient as you try to change."

On the other side, sometimes the most loving thing one can do for the other is to say—and mean—"I know it is hard for you to forgive and forget. I don't think you are trying to punish me or get even, and I shall try not to lose patience when you strike out at me with bitter, sarcastic words, or when you draw away from me."

The New Testament word for patience is a lovely one that means "long-tempered." That says a lot about what is needed in a relationship that is out of shape. If mending the brokenness is really important, "long-tempered" rather than "short-tempered" behavior is appropriate.

Kindness is the active side of patience. If patience is toleration of the other's floundering but honest efforts to act responsibly and redemptively, kindness is reaching out a helping hand. Patience says, "I will give you time and space to get yourself together." Kindness says, "We are partners in this thing. What can I do to help get us together?"

Patience sits back; kindness steps forward. Patience waits; kindness takes the initiative. Both are needed, for there is a time to keep silent and a time to speak up. There is a time to let the other person work out his problem, and a time to join him in solving it. The caring person seeks appropriate ways to make the patience-kindness response to his partner's need.

The capacity to trust and to be trustworthy is probably the most mature human achievement. To trust another for whom you care deeply is an evidence of your self-esteem, for you are saying, "I believe you value what we have together and will not want to damage it." Assuming that the other person cannot be trusted out of your sight betrays that you do not have a very high opinion of yourself.

Further, given the desire of the other to make the relationship a good one, trust inspires trustworthiness. We all have a way of meeting expectations. If we expect the other person to behave shabbily, we have given him an excuse to do so. If we expect him to behave responsibly, we have provided him an incentive—that is, if he is a decent person. If not, there is not much going for the relationship anyway.

Where trust has been violated it can be restored only by intensive effort of the wronged party to express confidence in the other's trustworthiness, and careful attention by the offending party to the need to be reassuring. If one says, "I'm not sure I can trust you," and the other says, "That's your problem," there will be no healing.

Only as each seeks to see the situation through the other's eyes is there a good prognosis for the relationship. Seeing life through another's eyes is a rare and precious gift—the gift of love. And that is what marriage and family are all about.

3

Is Marriage Obsolete?

"Marriage in its present condition is obsolete," distinguished author William J. Lederer concluded after interviews with more than six hundred married couples.

The couples were asked: "If you could wave a magic wand which would divorce you and your spouse immediately, without inconvenience, without suffering to anyone in the family, without social censure or expense, would you wave the magic wand and get a divorce?" Almost three-fourths of them, including the happily married and the unhappily married, answered "yes."

Divorce statistics dismay people who take seriously the biblical admonition: "What therefore God hath joined together, let not man put asunder" (Matt. 19:6, KJV). In the United States divorces now exceed one million a year. Soon we shall live in a society where one out of every three persons who marries will be divorced at least once during his lifetime.

The sexual revolution everybody talks about is no myth. The illegitimacy rate has almost doubled in this country since 1965, despite widespread availability of contraceptives. In 1976 there were 476,000 illegitimate births in the United States, more than one out of every seven. Nine out of ten unwed mothers get on welfare rolls, costing taxpayers billions of dollars a year.

HEW Secretary Joseph A. Califano, Jr. declared that sexual permissiveness leading to teenage pregnancy is "one of the most serious and complex problems facing our nation today." Each year, one out of ten girls between fifteen and nineteen, most of them unmarried, gets pregnant.

If church and school have nothing to say about sexual morality, who will speak? We are saturated by "sex-ploitation" from every source—television, rock and country music, movies, advertisements, fashions, and the example set by multitudes of folk heroes. Audiences no longer titter in embarrassment over comic references to fornication and adultery, but are titillated by thinly-veiled allusions to homosexuality and even bestiality. The human penchant for taking every stimulation to its ultimate expression is about to be realized with respect to sex. The folk wisdom of this age is the unabashed hedonism which says, "If it feels good, do it."

Where to begin with this phenomenon? Well, most people who read this are committed to biblical faith, if not to some church. The Bible does not regard marriage as a secular arrangement. To be sure, secularists marry and are faithful to their partners. Some believers who marry are unfaithful to their covenant. Nonetheless, marriage for us is a sacred covenant, not just with one's partner but also with God.

Much confusion about marriage arises from failure to insist that when a believer marries he has entered into a holy and irrevocable covenant. Primary and normative to Christian thinking is the covenantal nature of marriage.

Genesis 1 and 2 are full of meaning for those who believe in marriage as covenant. Although created in God's image, human beings are not complete and self-sufficient. God saw that "it is not good that the man should be alone" (Gen. 2:18, KJV). God recognized the need for marriage. It was as though the creation of human beings was unfinished work until a partnership relationship had been provided. So God made a helper for man. The Hebrew word for *helper* in no sense suggests an unequal or servile role for woman. She is not her husband's assistant, but his partner. She is, in the words of *Today's English Version* translation, "a suitable companion."

When she was brought to man he named her "woman," *ishah,* because she was taken out of man, *ish.* Her nature is the same as his, as she is made of the same stuff. Equal in creation, they are separate in function, each complementing the other. Only of man alone, without woman, did God declare that it was not good. "It is not good that the man should be alone," God said. Male-female is a polarity in which each completes the other, making the "not good" very good.

The two become one flesh, says Scripture, implying far more than the obvious joining of bodies in the sex act. Marriage is a merging of the male-female separate units into one corporate personality. The biblical understanding of marriage is not that two self-sufficient bodies establish certain points of union with one another, say at the mating level, the housing level, the child-rearing level. Biblical marriage is not a limited partnership designed to meet certain mutual needs while excluding mutual liability. Biblical marriage is total union, a merger in which each undertakes unconditional caring and responsibility for the other.

Whatever the secularizing of American life does to marriages of secularists, people of biblical faith are called to take seriously what the Bible says about marriage as a covenant relationship. Only so will marriage as we have known it not become obsolete.

4

On Behalf of the Unmarried

In the Bible marriage is normative. God made them male and female and said, "For this cause shall a man leave his father and mother and shall cleave to his wife" (Matt. 19:5, KJV). In the Old Testament there is no word for *bachelor*.

To have children to perpetuate one's name and family was a high priority for a Hebrew man. To be denied marriage was a great deprivation. One of the prophet Jeremiah's burdens was that God commanded him not to marry.

For a woman not to marry and bear children was a reproach. Isaiah describes the devastation of war with its decimation of the male population in the vivid figure of seven women clinging to one man and begging him to marry them in order to "take away our reproach" (Isa. 4:1, KJV).

But these are not Old Testament days, and it is inappropriate for the church and other helping institutions to take the attitude toward single people, "Get married or we have nothing for you." Singleness in our society is to be reckoned with.

Now more than six million "never-marrieds" forty and above live in this country. More than five million divorced persons and twelve million widowed persons live in the United States. Four-fifths of the widowed are female. Soon there will be fifty percent more women than men over age sixty-five. In 1973 one in every eight families in the United States was headed by a woman, and the figure is rising.

An important factor in the contemporary scene is women's emergence as partners with men in the human enterprise. Once women's relationships with men were largely confined to males in their families. That obviously and happily is no longer true. The male-female relationship is widely diverse, often as not having nothing to do with romance or sexual behavior.

The assumption that the only proper place for a woman to be womanly is in the safe confines of the home is as absurd as the notion that the only appropriate role for a man is husband and father. Men are male human beings who may or may not marry and father children; women are female human beings who may or may not marry and bear children. Until women are free to be persons with the unique gifts of femaleness and not sex objects, and men are free to be persons and not male predators, we shall go on behaving as if the only way for men and women to be safe with one another is to get married to legitimize their sexual desires.

Jesus seems not to have had any qualms about associating with unmarried women. It seems certain that two of his closest friends, Mary and Martha, were single. So apparently was Mary Magdalene. In fact, one of the Gospels says candidly that women accompanied and ministered to Jesus.

Paul unjustly has received rough treatment from many who call him a male chauvinist. But Paul greatly respected women, sent special greetings to some of his female friends in his letters, and relied upon them for help. How can Paul be anti-feminist when he wrote that in Christ "there is neither male nor female" (Gal. 3:28, KJV)? He honored the unmarried and was unmarried himself, as was Barnabas, another apostle. It seems certain that our Lord was unmarried. We assume so only from the silence of Scripture, not because marriage would have soiled him in some manner.

Indeed, marriage is "an honorable estate," as the marriage service reads. But so is singleness. We must stop making single persons feel they need to apologize. One of the most denigrating things we marrieds do is to be smugly patronizing toward those who "didn't make it or couldn't keep it."

An unmarried pastor writes: "We are beginning at the wrong place to discuss the single life-style or the married life-style as the basis for a Christian life-style. The Bible doesn't begin there at all. God is first of all much more interested that we are his than whether we are married or single." A single professional woman writes, "I am not a frustrated female who wishes that the Lord had made her a man. I am happy being a woman. I like women except when they are whining about either being married or being single, or when the married ones give me the 'you-poor-darling-you're-not-married' treatment."

All persons, single or married, need to realize that environment is an echo chamber which answers us with the sounds we ourselves make. If we make happy, self-affirming sounds, that is what we shall hear. If we make despairing, self-pitying sounds, the whole world is one enormous wail. To paraphrase Shakespeare, it is not in our marital state but in ourselves that we are underlings—if we are.

5

The Art of Parenting

Nothing more inspires comments on parenting than two weeks in an automobile across country with grandchildren. Safely home, I am full of advice—and relief. I jest. Ours are most unusual grandchildren. Would any grandparent disagree?

The night after we flew home, leaving them in San Francisco to drive back across the continent, they called and the six-year-old said, "Pop, you missed the highlight of the trip today. I threw up in the car." Sorry I wasn't there.

I like the way my grandchildren are being brought up. Talking with their parents, we came up with "Ten Commandments of Successful Parenting." See what you think about them.

1. *Thou Shalt Structure Flexibly.* Children who grow up without structure, without rules, without fences, are victims of a frightful tyranny. Thank God, we do not live in a structureless universe, a capricious environment. Everybody needs struc-

ture, especially children. Permissive child rearing is a manifestly silly notion. At the same time, rules should be flexible. To say to a child, "You go to bed at eight o'clock, regardless of the circumstances," is a little ridiculous. Rules untempered by common sense, are tyranny. Rules which are nonnegotiable are also a form of tyranny.

2. *Thou Shalt Love Unconditionally.* The child's only essential security is the knowledge of his parents' unconditional love. If he has that he can endure almost any other deprivation without being emotionally crippled. Conditional love says, "We love you if and when ... you say 'yes, sir' and 'no, sir' to your father; bring home good grades; don't talk back or argue; are polite to your grandparents; etc., etc." Unconditional love never links the giving of love with performance. Genuine love is a given and a constant. It does not say, "I love you because." It says simply, "I love you. You are precious to me. Nothing you do or fail to do makes me love you more or less. I love you. You are my child."

The happy, secure child has had such unconditional acceptance communicated. The insecure child senses that approval from the most important people in his life—parents—depends upon his meeting their expectations. That is a tough role to play in life.

3. *Thou Shalt Discipline Appropriately.* The clue to healthy discipline is to remember that the word's basic meaning is *teaching.* Granted the need for it, is the discipline instructive or punitive? Are we helping the child to understand not only that his behavior displeases us, but why we consider it unacceptable? Or are we merely dealing with our own anger and frustration, abusing the child verbally or physically, or both, because we are bigger and stronger?

Spanking may be appropriate, but deprivation of privileges may be more effective. Having done a bit of both in my time as a parent, I suspect that laying on of hands was more often a display of my own anger than sensible dealing with the child's behavior. The bottom line in discipline is, "Did the child learn anything that will help him/her grow into a responsible, decision-making adult?"

4. *Thou Shalt Explain Fully.* The world is one great mystery made up of a thousand, thousand wonders. The child's mind is a thirsty sponge ready and able to soak up limitless amounts of information, experience, feelings. But who will tell him about the mystery? Who better than the parent? If "You never told me that you love me" is the worst thing a child can say to his parent, the next worse is "You never explained anything to me or took time to teach me anything."

Think how fortunate you are to have a child's rapt attention, face glued to yours, as you share with him or her the commonplace wonders of the world God put together and made available for our enjoyment. Remember, too, the interior world of your own beliefs, hopes, spiritual experience. Wouldn't it be sad to think that the greatest mystery of all mysteries to your child is you?

5. *Thou Shalt Praise Generously.* Most of us are more verbal with complaint and criticism than we are with gratitude and commendation. We can say what displeases us, but we are tongue-tied when the opportunity to affirm arises. The child's experience is enriched by the quality of the little kindnesses of parental approval. "You look pretty in that dress." "What a handsome son I have!" Thank you for helping." "What a nice job you did cleaning your room!" In my work with college students I have realized as I never did with my own children that parents have the power to bless or curse their children as does no one else. To withhold approval and affirmation is to curse your child.

6. *Thou Shalt Show Affection Warmly.* You may love without showing affection. Wholesome food, warm shelter and clothing, and an invigorating social environment are all ways of loving. But for the child they are sterile if unaccompanied by affection.

Children also need to see their parents show affection for each other. The child with parents who are affectionate feels good about himself. After all, he is a product of both of them. If they like one another it is easy for him to like himself, inasmuch as the two parts of himself like one another. Further, parents who are affectionate with their children, free to hug, kiss, and cuddle them, help their children to grow healthy feelings about their own bodies and their need to be close to someone they love. The child deprived of being held close by his parents may become a cold, stiff-arming adult. Or he may become an emotionally sick grown-up who only knows how to relate to other people by hopping from bed to bed.

7. *Thou Shalt Listen Closely.* Too often the image of a good parent-child relationship is the child sitting quietly at the parent's knee while the parent imparts wisdom, instruction, or admonition. There is no human interaction. The child would be about as well off sent to his room with a record of Dr. Seuss.

Parent, how much do you listen to your children? Are your conversations with them little more than lectures by you, the fount of all wisdom? Do you catch yourself being annoyed when they want to tell you something that seems trivial to you but may be earthshaking to them? Do you snap impatiently, "Can't you see I'm reading—or watching the evening news—or talking?" Do you say, "Don't interrupt. Have you no manners?"

The God-given art of speech is one of the richest resources human beings have for reaching out to others. How can children learn to talk with other people if they are discouraged from discussing ideas, feelings, and beliefs with their parents?

8. *When Thou Art Wrong Admit It Readily.* About the hardest sentence in the English language is, "I'm sorry, I was wrong." Husbands and wives have a terrible time saying it to one another, and parents have even more trouble saying it to their children. Why are we so threatened by admitting a mistake, an error in judgment, a boo-boo? Why must we be omni-

scient? Do we really think we are God? Do we lose face saying "I was wrong," or by maintaining a position that is indefensible? Which do you suppose your child respects?

9. *Thou Shalt Model Carefully.* "What you do speaks so loudly that I can't hear what you say" was never so true as in the child's relationship with his parent. When I think of parental example I think of King David in the Bible. Every weakness and foible he had came home to roost in the behavior of his children. So often it does. We sow the wind and reap the whirlwind. But the positive side is also true. We sow seed and reap a harvest a hundredfold. Be careful what you sow, for "that [you] shall . . . also reap" (Gal. 6:7, KJV).

10. *Thou Shalt Choose Your Environment Prayerfully.* If you want your children to be good people, associate with good people. If you care whether they love God and serve him, involve your family with the family of God in a church. You can't live a materialistic, pagan life yourself and expect that your children are going to grow up loving God and his kingdom.

More than that, the parent who pays no attention to the kind of company his child keeps either doesn't care what happens to him or is a blind fool. Jesus said, "Judge not," but in the same conversation he also said, "Do not give dogs what is holy"; and "Do not throw your pearls before swine" (Matt. 7:1,6, RSV). The pearl of great price, the holiest of holies, is the life of your child. If you don't know who his/her friends are you had better find out quickly. All your love and care may be destroyed by a depraved, drug-controlled, value-vacuum environment.

When Eve bore her first son she said, "I have gotten a man with the help of the Lord" (Gen. 4:1, RSV). We people of biblical faith believe that the Lord is indeed a partner in the enterprise of parenting.

6

When Love Is Strong

Much that passes for love is sentimentality with the consistency of a marshmallow. I am afraid it may be the product of bad sermons and poor Bible teaching.

Love is misunderstood when interpreted as passive resignation to imposition from others. "Love bears all things," we quote from Paul's immortal 1 Corinthians 13:7, and then misinterpret him by saying that love has no self-respect and requires nothing of others. Whatever else love is, it is not a doormat.

Counselors see people in trouble, and often the trouble relates to a misunderstanding of the obligation to love. Here is a husband or wife who offers only passive resistance to thoughtless, selfish exploitation by the marriage partner. Resentment and anger emerge in physical distress and depression. But because of "love," the one being destroyed cannot face up to what is happening and demand changes.

Or here is a parent who permits a child to tyrannize and intimidate the entire family. Other family members are imposed upon, love and care taken for granted, and the home used as a convenience without investment of time, love, or concern in return. Too often I see intelligent, godly, middle-aged adults who are afraid to confront selfish, spoiled and irresponsible adolescents for fear of appearing unloving.

Or here is a concerned, sensitive student whose roommate or friend drains him emotionally with ceaseless demands for support and reassurance. Like enormous thirsty sponges such people can never be satisfied. Loving friends, disturbed by the other's chronic unhappiness, or periodically alarmed by threats to end it all, live in ceaseless consternation and self-reproach because they are unable to give enough to the other person.

In all such cases there is a basic fallacy about love. It is that love never says "No," never stands up for itself, never lets its expectations and needs be clearly known to the other. That is pseudolove, disguised as concern, but masking unwillingness to risk loving the other enough to let him see how we really perceive him and ourselves. Genuine love is the strong quality that cares so much about the other person that it wants him to know who you are and who he is, and to achieve mature personhood in the light of those perceptions.

The spouse who passively accepts being treated as a convenience is not acting in love, but perpetuating selfish immaturity in the partner and preventing him from ever perceiving himself or his spouse as a mature and responsible person. The parents who permit their children to use and abuse them are teaching them bad lessons. Where are they going to find other people who will tolerate their abominable behavior? The student who allows a roommate or friend to absorb and manipulate their life is not a true friend. Better to have a crisis now than to have it later, or to let him go through life searching for victims.

Love is not weakness, but strength. Love does not reject, but neither does it passively accept exploitation. That is destructive both to the exploited and the exploiter. Jesus put this plainly: "If your brother [wrongs you], rebuke him; and if he repents, forgive him" (Luke 17:3, RSV).

That is strong. It takes character to rebuke your brother when he has wronged you. Passive resentment and self-despising are much easier. But it also takes character to forgive if your brother repents. And Jesus said that this kind of rebuking and forgiving love must go on and on. There is to be no limit to the relationship from love's side so long as wrong is met with rebuke and repentance with forgiveness. Our problem often is that we don't know how to do either—rebuke or forgive.

VII

Turning On or Tuning In

1

Putting Practice into Theory

My grandfather was a salt-of-the-earth farmer with little schooling and a lot of sense. He knew more about people than many a Ph.D. with fancy names for ordinary human foibles.

Grandfather told about a man who got religion after being a notorious carouser. The change was so dramatic that he was always being asked to tell how he got saved. He was so impressed with himself that he wrote out his experience and stored the paper in the attic for posterity.

A new preacher came to call and the convert's wife went to the attic to fetch the paper. Momentarily she came bounding down the stairs and burst into the parlor, aghast. "Mice in the attic," she announced "have eaten up your experience."

That happens to fresh, vital, firsthand experiences which are allowed to become no more than memories to be preserved and occasionally rehearsed but never renewed and reexperienced. The history of a movement usually has four parts: (1) event; (2) report; (3) standardization; (4) regimentation.

First, something exciting happens and people get caught up in it. Then they spread the word. Next, tests are introduced to make sure the story is told right, and there get to be orthodox and unorthodox ways of telling the story. Finally, those powerful enough to designate their story as the orthodox one enforce it upon everybody they can.

The history of Christianity can be written in that framework. Something incredibly exciting happened! One of them wrote it out like this: "We have not depended on made-up stories in making known to you the mighty coming of our Lord Jesus Christ. With our own eyes we saw his greatness."

They were not made-up stories. People shared what had happened, and when they did they could report it only as they understood it. But every person is unique and, therefore, no report was a carbon copy of another. All reports of events are in some measure interpretations of the event. All statements of faith are editorials, including this one.

Since the report of the event is subject to what the reporter brings to the event, how can one be sure there is a standard by which to interpret the event? That issue produced the New Testament. Something happened—something wonderful, miraculous—and they were compelled to report it. But how can we be sure that the report was not altered through repetition and the passage of time? And how can we ascertain the meaning of the report? We come to a point of faith and judge that God inspired the reporters and directed the men who finally determined which reports should make up the New Testament.

The New Testament is, therefore, a "good news" report, giving an interpretation of the meaning of Jesus Christ. It is also a manual on how to conduct one's life in the light of the divine event. If one has been spiritually changed by the event, one's manner of life should reflect certain behavior, such as "love, joy, peace, patience, kindness, goodness, faithfulness, gentleness, self-control" (Gal. 5:22, RSV).

The last stage of any great movement is regimentation or coercion. From event to report to standardization to regulation is the history of most great events. Once we have decided the orthodox meaning of the event, we begin to insist that everybody experience and report the event alike.

"Faith" becomes "the faith." The norm is no longer "Have you believed?" but "Do you believe what we tell you to believe?" Those who do not are heretics and revisionists. The history of Christendom has dark chapters of the harassment, persecution, and martyrdom of persons who did not understand their experience of God in the way they were required to do.

What happens to a movement happens in individual experience also. Something crucial happens to us, and we feel the need to tell other people about it. But we also need to understand it, figure out its implications. Thus, we tend to standardize it, categorize it, explain its meaning. Thereafter, unless we are perceptive and humble, we tend to judge others' experience by whether or not it matches our own.

That is the risk of putting practice into theory. There is no way totally to avoid running that risk. All four of the parts of experience are valid: having the experience, talking about it, evaluating or interpreting it, and urging it upon other people.

2

On Losing Your Religion

Remember the old jest about a trying situation: "It just about made me lose my religion!" The truth is that many do lose their religion, at least for periods in life. Traditional religion is all some people have, and it won't survive the first serious test it faces. Secondhand religion, Mama's religion, often only Sunday School religion, is unexamined religion, with all the facets of a protected environment. Christ in such religion is captive of culture and region. But inherited religion is not faith. Like a cut flower it wilts and shatters. It has no way of renewing itself, and lasts only as long as it is refrigerated away from the challenging atmosphere of everyday life.

People with secondhand faith are terribly vulnerable to harsh reality, for when they need honest-to-goodness faith in God in time of trouble or stress, they have nothing. Secondhand religion usually doesn't survive the first year in college, or the first big temptation, or the first deep grief.

Religion also easily lost is the "just-believe" brand which raises no significant question about God or what he might be saying to us. "I-just-believe" religion operates on the theory that life is full of mystery, and one should assign to God what cannot be accounted for otherwise. God's department is what we can't figure out or manage by ourselves. Thus God becomes the divine emergency exit.

Neither will religion that is little more than pious sentimentalism, popular religion, survive the long pull. Jesus once replied sharply to a man making a sentimental response to him, "The Son of man has nowhere to lay his head" (Matt. 8:20, RSV). Shallow sentimentalism can get equally emotional over an old

TV movie or a powerful sermon, but it won't do anything about either. It gets moist-eyed from singing, "Wherever He Leads I'll Go," but it won't go around the block—let alone around the world—to help somebody in need. Such religion has its meaning not in the reality of God but in one's feelings. When feelings alter there is no substance left.

Another variety of perishable religion is "religion-in-general," which avoids specific beliefs and commitments. The confession of faith usually begins: "I don't subscribe to any particular faith. I think that they are all saying basically the same thing. My creed is to do the best I can." Sometimes the Golden Rule is invoked. This is be-nice-to-old-people-and-animals religion. It doesn't object to religious institutions, thinking them to be useful to community life, but it does not intend to be involved. It is like being in favor of education but not wanting to support schools.

Some folks don't have much religion to lose. And some religion ought to be lost. It isn't worth keeping.

3

Comforting or Comfortable Religion

Our biblical faith has a strong note of comfort in it. "Comfort ye, comfort ye my people, saith your God" (Isa. 40:1, KJV), wrote one of the prophets. There is forgiveness as well as rebuke. There is chastisement, but there is also consolation, and never the first without the second unless the first is ignored, in which case the second is pointless.

Paul, who knew how to chastise with a sharp tongue, knew also how to comfort. Once he wrote this doxology: "Blessed be the God and Father of our Lord Jesus Christ, the Father of mercies and God of all comfort, who comforts us in all our affliction, so that we may be able to comfort those who are in any affliction, with the comfort with which we ourselves are comforted by God" (2 Cor. 1:3-4, RSV).

The style is a bit involved, but the meaning is not in doubt. God is not only Lord of creation, not only Sovereign of history, holding in his hand the schedule of civilizations. He is the God of all comfort, comforting us in all our affliction.

Afflictions surround our lives. Some have to do with frustration of our understanding. We are quite unable to grasp the meaning of existence. There are altogether too many unanswered and unanswerable whys. Questions of meaning; reasons for undeserved suffering, defeat and death; the inability of man to live with his fellows on this miraculous green ball of earth; the hope for life beyond the grave.

Another affliction is our aloneness, our sense of isolation and estrangement from others. How often do we say, "No one understands me; no one really cares." People with problems nearly always sense isolation. Much of the nonsense that goes on in our society in the name of "being sociable" has its source in the need to break through the insulation.

A third affliction is the meaning of the work we do. What assurance do we have that what we are doing is worth the effort? Is it the nagging fear that it may not have any lasting meaning which produces such negative attitudes toward work in our society?

Pressure confounds us all in the realization of our moral incompetence, our incredible folly, our weakness of will, our sin. If all that is necessary to ensure the living of a good life were the understanding of its nature, things would be simpler. Tragically, we know better than we are. Our will is unequal to our knowledge.

Paul argues that there is divine help available for "afflictions." He makes a bold promise. "God ... comforts us in all our afflictions." Had God comforted him? Yes, again and again. Paul had been on the edge of the abyss more than once. He was writing out of personal experience.

But what had God done for him? He had "comforted" him. The word means *fortify*. God had fortified him. God had not taken away the afflictions, the pressures. He had built up Paul's inner fortifications to bear them.

That is the difference between "comfortable" and "comforting" religion. Comfortable religion seduces you, tells you to relax and be satisfied just the way you are. Comforting religion encourages you to believe in the possibilities which you have not yet realized.

Comfortable religion tells you not to think about things that are disturbing or upsetting. Comforting religion makes you uneasy about injustice and suffering, even if it is somebody else's.

Comfortable religion talks about how "the Lord has blessed us, our church, our nation," and encourages you to feel smug about it. Comforting religion reminds you that "to whom much is given, of him shall much be required" (Luke 12:48, RSV).

Comfortable religion turns your attention in upon yourself. Comforting religion challenges you to quit thinking about yourself so much and begin looking at other people's needs.

Comfortable religion is soft, smooth, unabrasive. Comforting religion is strong, rugged, salty.

Comfortable religion encourages dependency. Comforting religion, interdependency.

Comfortable religion encourages you to protect yourself from the world's harshness. Comforting religion equips you to deal with it without despair or destructive anger.

God is the God of comfort, but not of cushions.

4

Turning On or Tuning In

Some people get turned on intellectually to religion. They really enjoy the mental stimulation of religious talk. They get caught up in comparing this theory with that, or this religious system with another.

Paul, the missionary, went to Athens, Greece, in the middle of the first century AD and discovered that the discussion of religion was one of the liveliest games in town. The philosophers even had a place where they gathered to discuss it. Further, shrines and statues in the names of all the gods imaginable could be seen on the streets. Athens was a community bursting with religious interest.

But Paul wanted to reveal a consuming, passionate faith that God had entered human history through Jesus Christ and in Christ's death and resurrection was the potential for a new world. Paul found minimal response to the claim that religion ought to make a decisive difference in the way one views life and lives it. To the Athenians it was only an interesting subject for clever minds.

Jesus often made the same distinction between good and bad religion. "Why do you call me 'Lord, Lord,' " he asked "and do not do the things I say?" (Luke 6:46). What did he say to do? "Feed the hungry, clothe the naked, visit the sick and imprisoned" (Matt. 25:35-36).

"Turn on" religion intrigues the mind or vents the emotions without responsibly engaging the will. Religion may be only a pious form of narcissism which sings with delight, "Oh, that will be glory for me!" Do we really worship God or do we like him because he helps us to feel good about ourselves? What are we saying about our understanding of God and our commitment to him if we are always concentrating on our own happiness?

"Turn on" religion may be nothing more than sentimentalism covered with a thin veneer of piety. With the world so terrible a place, the refuge of religion is most attractive. We can run and hide behind God's chair. Well, there is biblical support for such use of religion. "God is our refuge and strength,/a very present help in trouble" (Ps. 46:1, RSV).

But there is danger in it, too. Religion can be a subtle drug, making us feel warm and cozy, narcotizing us against the pain we would feel at the sight and sound of our brother's plight. We like to feel good, and "mood" religion with its soft lights, gentle music, and soothing sermons helps us to do that.

On the other hand the prophetic word disturbs us, challenges our complacency and lack of involvement in humanity's hurts. When religion becomes an insulation between us and another's need it has become an enemy of God.

I don't mean to put down those who enjoy their religion or are glad to witness to the deliverance they have experienced. Quite the contrary. What I am pointing out is the need to tune it in.

Work on getting into focus what you mean when you claim to have a religious commitment. What is the basis of your belief? What difference does it make in the way you live? Would you live any differently if you did not hold to the belief you claim? I am asking for religion that is tuned in to the human situation. Religion that allows you always to be gloriously happy and does not ever cause you to feel the pain of the world is suspect.

The prophet Amos, 750 years before Christ, announced God's woe to those who lived in the lap of luxury. They slept on beds inlaid with ivory, eating and drinking to their gluttonous content, but were not "grieved over the ruin of Joseph" (an expression to mean their brothers; Amos 6:6, RSV). How can anyone claim that God has taken hold of him and made him sensitive and aware if he shows no grief over the ruin of his brothers? Is God not grieved?

But it is not enough to feel sorry. That can be a futile short-circuiting of action. Tune in your concern to some specific need and see what you can do to make it better. Tune out the impulses which tell you to think about yourself or to take religious fancy flights away from the world scene about you.

Listen to the words of Albert Schweitzer: "However much I was concerned at the problem of the misery in the world, I never let myself get lost in broodings over it; I always held firmly to the thought that each one of us can do a little to bring some portion of it to an end."

5

The Meaning-Monger

Dr. Dean M. Kelley, a church official, got to wondering a few years ago why some churches are declining and others are rapidly growing. The more he studied this religious phenomenon the more convinced he became that the essential ingredients of a successful religious appeal are: (1) convincing answers to the meaning of life, and, (2) demands for commitment to the answers.

Churches with declining attendance, lower recruitment figures, and budget crises were frequently the very ones which might have been expected to attract moderns. They were affluent, educated, refined, urbane, and sophisticated. They offered entertainment, recreation, fine facilities, and a liberal attitude toward social practices. The only thing they had less of year after year was people.

Other churches, often outwardly unattractive, sometimes with a poorly-educated ministry, unusual rituals, peculiar dietary customs, narrow-minded disregard for the views of others, and strict imposition of uniformity in belief and behavior, were flourishing. They had few characteristics generally believed essential to a successful, modern American movement. The only thing they had was people—lots and lots of people.

How to explain this apparent anomaly? Kelley suspected that failure or success had little to do with facilities, programs, slogans, or educated staff, but with the absence or presence of a profound sense of meaning. The growing church was marked by a positive claim to have the answer to what life means, and also made strong demands for acquiescence to the answer. Of such churches Kelley wrote, "They remind us that man is an incorrigibly religious creature who wants to make sense out of his life. Man is an inveterate meaning-monger."

Declining churches tended to be less dogmatic about what they were saying, less positive that theirs was the "answer" to the questions of meaning. Broad-mindedness became the supreme virtue and intolerance the unpardonable sin. Floundering in such an ocean of relativity, people swim to the nearest lifeboat. The boat may be uncomfortable and unattractive, filled with people who have little interest in philosophical gamesmanship about the possibility of other and better lifeboats. But when the options are the lifeboat or the sea, there isn't much choice.

A crisis in meaning afflicts our age. The many ways in which people behave antisocially are symptomatic of the meaning-crisis. Boredom, addiction, alienation, depression, suicide, criminality, sexual aberration—all are meaning-maladies. People have no core, no stackpole in their lives around which they can arrange their values.

The declining church, Kelley observed, was uncomfortable saying to its people, "This is the way, walk ye in it" (Isa. 30:21, KJV). In place of dogma it substituted discussion, inviting people to play verbal table tennis with religious ideas. Religion as a church parlor game has little drawing power. People would prefer bridge or bingo.

Churches which draw people are those grappling with life-and-death issues and offering more than observations about the struggle. People want answers which provide a sense of coherence to their existence, and they will look until they find someone who offers them. The answers may seem absurd, even dangerous, to outsiders, but to those inside, they provide the essential structure to hold life together.

Wherever the "pearl of great price" (Matt. 13:46, KJV), as Jesus once termed the kingdom of God, is being offered in exchange for bits of loyalty and time plus pocket change, there are few takers. There is something contradictory and basically dishonest about such a "bargain." If it costs nothing, it can't be worth much. That is why churches making stringent demands are growing. Total commitment is the only appropriate response to salvation. If I have found the secret that explains the meaning of my existence I will cling to it tenaciously, and maintain it at whatever cost.

Further, if I believe that my "secret" holds the key to meaning, I shall feel impelled to share it with others I care for. Thus Dr. Kelley concluded that "strong churches" were always characterized by commitment, discipline, zeal, absolutism, conformity, and fanaticism. The intolerance implied by some of those words troubles us. But, says Kelley, "For twenty years I have been looking for one clear case that would disprove this theory. I have not as yet found one."

Certain conclusions seem inescapable. First, nobody survives very long in a sea of meaninglessness. Second, it becomes crucial that constructive systems be available, else people will embrace the first "gospel" that comes along, regardless of its nature. Finally, in order to preserve the pluralistic system that is the genius of America, we have to hope that people can find meaning without the absolutism and fanaticism which so often mark the zealot. Human beings require meaning.

6

What Is Church?

Church folks often act as though the Lord is not involved in the church. He said, "I will build my church" (Matt. 16:18), but we listen to the words and then say, "Now let's get on with the program." The church is his, but we behave as if it were ours and that we have to save it if it is to be saved. Pastors talk about "my people," and laymen make pronouncements about "such and such is not going to happen in our church." That is foreign to the New Testament, which plainly claims that the church is Christ's, and we are privileged to enjoy its shelter. Paul even calls the church Christ's body, Christ being the head.

Look closely at the models we admire and copy to build the church. One is the dollars-and-square-footage model. "We've got a great church," someone says. "We have a two-million-dollar plant and a half-a-million-dollar annual budget." How does that make a great church? General Motors makes that operation look like a peanut stand.

Another model is based on numbers. "The Lord is really blessing. We run twenty buses all over town and last Sunday we had 900 in Sunday School." On most any fall Saturday afternoon, 100,000 people will pile into a stadium and yell like fans—fanatics—at a football game. That beats any crowd I ever preached to—by a few thousand. Jesus's numbers once dwindled to twelve, and he said to the ones left, "Will ye also go away?" (John 6:67, KJV).

We try to build the church by using the "it's-us-against-them" model. In this operation we appeal to people's natural inclination to rivalry, suspicion, envy, prejudice, or arrogance. We are either the persecuted minority or the only ones who have the truth, and we have to conquer the enemy—others. We build by tearing others down.

We may choose the "don't-we-have-fun" model of ministry, seeking to build the church by reminding people continually how much fun it is to be a member of this group, the fellowship of excitement. Everything is super, nothing is just plain good, not to mention ordinary.

Then there is the "circus" model of church, based on sensational thrills. Many churches run their affairs on the principle that Jesus really should have jumped from the pinnacle of the Temple when he was so tempted. That would have drawn a crowd.

The "new product" model is a useful gimmick for building a religious group, and calling it *church*. Here we rely upon the appeal of the novel, count on the new to attract, rather than depending upon the Spirit to renew what we already have and are.

Last of all, if everything else fails, we have the "guilt trip" model. We can easily hook into people's guilt and make them feel rotten for not supporting the program, or proud of themselves if they do. We all know how to get at one another through guilt, and we all have enough of it to make it a powerful force.

But the New Testament is strangely silent about any and all of these hints for building the church. Jesus said: "I will build my church." How did he propose to do it? The New Testament model is really quite simple. The church is built by witness and nurture, both under the direction of the Spirit of the Lord. There is no primary and secondary order of these two, for to try to put one before the other is to do the chicken-and-egg riddle. Proclamation and cultivation are equally essential.

The favorite New Testament model for church is the family, a witnessing family—not a closed, exclusive, elitist family, but one which says, "Come, whoever you are, let us share with you the most wonderful news of what God has done."

The church that sees itself as a family of witnesses whose intention is to make its secret available to all who will hear is a New Testament church, provided that it also sees itself as a family nurturing all who seek its name and identity as their own. When does a family nurture? It nurtures when it affirms, teaches, corrects, forgives, shares, consoles, and provides a place and a name for its members.

7

A Voice or an Echo

If anyone ever asks you whether organized religion is a voice or an echo in society, tell him "Yes." An unbiased review of where religion has been to where it is in relation to the culture will lead one without an axe to grind to the conclusion that religion is both voice and echo. Another way of putting it is that the more comfortable a religious movement becomes in its social and economic environment, the more it takes upon itself the marks of its surroundings.

Our common ancestor, Israel, is a paradigm of the religious experience. Once she was no people, with wilderness for a home, pilgrimage for a vocation, and the hope of a Promised Land for a meaning. Then when the hope became reality, a new kind of peril emerged, far more dangerous than the threat of extermination by her enemies. It was the evaporation of her sense of mission, the homogenization of her uniqueness. Israel's voice might become an echo of Canaanite culture.

Most American churches fit that paradigm. Born in hardship, we have grown comfortable, no longer having to struggle for survival. Born a slave and an outcast, we have become respectable. Born powerless, we have become influential. Born poor, we have become wealthy. Born with a burning vision that enthralled us, we have become polite, affable, polished. Everyone sent forth to be salt is tempted to lose his savor.

Nearly every established denomination was at one time and in some place a persecuted minority, having its beginnings among those who "Marched to the beat of a different drummer." Denied the right to preach and to worship, religious leaders went to jail for defying what they believed to be laws contrary to the law of God. They engaged in civil disobedience, willingly taking the consequences, declaring that they would rot in jail before acknowledging the right of the state to tell them when and if they could preach the gospel. We bask in the glow of their burning devotion to religious liberty, and we can do so with the comfortable luxury of never having to fuel that fire with our own defiance of public opinion or the law. We do not have to resist the establishment, for we are the establishment.

An inescapable question arises. Has the social order become so much like the kingdom of God that there is no longer any significant tension between the world and the church? "Are there no foes for me to fight? Must I not stem the flood?" Has the world become like the church or the church like the world? Probably a good deal of both.

The crime of human slavery and the Southern church's acquiescence in it in American history makes us wonder about the prophetic voice of organized religion. Not all white Southern church members either held slaves or supported slavery. Only a small minority owned slaves, but such persons were wealthy, landowning, and powerful. They largely controlled the institutions of the South, including the churches which became largely an echo on the slave issue. Sermons "proved" that slavery had biblical sanction and that slaves in America were better off than "heathens" in Africa who had not been delivered from the bondage of sin.

After the Civil War churches continued to reflect the cultural pattern by maintaining largely segregated churches. There isn't much evidence to show that we churchmen were seriously bothered by Jim Crowism until the issue of racial justice was forcibly called to our attention by black people and the courts. Then many of us "got religion."

Our record is spotty in other places, too. A doctoral dissertation on this issue reported recently that "any relation between Christian morality and economic justice" is hard to find in the editorials in religious journals of my own denomination. One critic says of us, "The church is in the world in the sense that the pastor prays at the PTA and the football game." That smarts. It is a caricature, but most caricatures are based upon a real defect.

The church in the world is always in the tension between being a voice and an echo. Being a voice takes faith, insight and courage. It can also be costly. But to become an echo is to cease being church at all.

8

How to Minister to Your Minister

Do you ever wonder who pastors your pastor? Who feeds his soul—which is not the same as feeding his ego—as he feeds yours? Who gives him the affirmation of his "alrightness," encouraging him to believe that his life has meaning?

I can hear you protesting. "We pay him to do those things for us!"

"He is supposed to be a man of God, not like us. He shouldn't have those needs."

"I do not have a pastor; as a matter of fact, I don't even like preachers. They are creeps who lay guilt on you and take your money."

Well, now, let me tell you something about pastors. I have been on both sides of the pastor-pastored fence. I was a pastor, then a professor, then a pastor again, and for the last dozen years have been a chaplain and professor again. Pastors are human, too. They put on their pants like anybody else. As Shakespeare's Shylock said, "If you prick us, do we not bleed? If you tickle us, do we not laugh?"

Some people only like their pastor as long as he is new and they don't know him. They never get beyond the novelty stage of the relationship, but regularly go down the scale from an ecstatic and unrealistic "Oh, he's marvelous" to "Oh, he's all right" to "Oh, he's a good man, but" to "Oh Lord, how long?"

If you want to pastor your pastor, don't expect the impossible of him. He is not the Lord or Superman. Most ministers know that, and they desperately need parishioners who are also aware of it. Once in a while you run into a minister who acts like Little Lord Fauntleroy, but most of them are decent people trying very hard to serve God by ministering to God's people.

Don't make omniscience part of his job description, for hardly anybody qualifies. Don't expect him to know everything, even about God, and don't encourage him to talk as if he does. Both he and you are in trouble when he begins to say, "My job is to tell you what is the will of God," instead of, "Let us seek God's will together."

Let him be human. He can't stay on duty twenty-four hours a day and survive. He needs to be able to take off his clerical collar. Let him have friends within his congregation if he chooses, people with whom he can be just plain Bill. If you are not his fishing or golfing buddy, don't be jealous and pout. Only God is up to loving everybody with equal intensity. Pastors live lonely lives if they are made to feel that they should never make friends within their church family.

Don't expect his wife to be the unpaid assistant pastor and his children to be miniature pastors. His family will most probably feel good about the church in direct ratio to the church's acceptance of the family as normal human beings.

Encourage in him, in yourself, and in your church, the conviction that he is a man chosen by God to minister. His task is to show and tell God's boundless love and grace. He does this by the way he lives, as well as by the way he preaches and teaches. He comforts you in pain and sorrow, he admonishes you in your sin, never suggesting that he is invulnerable to pain or above sin. Let him be what he is—prophet, pastor, and friend.

Pray for him, as you hope he prays for you. If he is worth his salt, he will be thankful for a parishioner who believes that much in God and cares that much for his pastor. And he will be the first to tell you that he needs it.

Enable him to live with dignity. Don't make him beg for his living, or lick your hand like a puppy after a crumb. Apply the Golden Rule—treat him as you wish to be treated. He likely works longer hours than most people in his congregation, and he doesn't mind doing it. If he is any good he could make more money doing something else, but he wouldn't trade places with anybody.

Don't fawn over him, either. Don't turn him into a sycophant or a popinjay. Just let him be a human being with a special calling and training for his task. He won't be perfect, and if he were, you couldn't stand him. Remember what religious people did to God's Son.

VIII

A Satisfactory Friend

1

God Does Not Want Perpetual Infants

A girl walked in, slammed her books down in disgust, and fumed, "I just blew my math test."

"Oh," I said reassuringly, "maybe you did better than you think."

"No way," she said with a finality that suggested another tack might be more productive.

"It's not the end of the world," I offered.

She just looked at me. I knew better than to have said that. She didn't need me to tell her it wasn't the end of the world.

"What makes me so furious," she explained, "is that as I was walking down the hall this guy caught up with me and asked how I did on the test. When I told him I had messed it up he said that he had aced it.

"That wouldn't have been so bad," she went on, "but he was bragging about how little he had studied for it. I had knocked myself out reviewing. He told me that when he looked over the test he couldn't work a single problem, so he just bowed his head and said, 'Lord, you've got to give me the answers,' and the Lord made his *A* for him."

I wanted to throw up. The only reasonable conclusion to such religious nonsense is that colleges do not need math departments to teach students how to do math problems. All students really need is to be taught to ask the Lord to give them the answers. Can we not find a way to believe in God, to believe in prayer, and to believe in miracles without making a mockery of intelligence?

Great effort is required for the human animal to mature. Little is given automatically. Behavior is learned, often painfully. Hocking wrote about man that of all animals he is the one in whom heredity counts for least. "Other creatures nature could largely finish—the human creature must finish himself."

If God permits us to be perpetual infants, spoon-fed all our lives, all we have to do is learn how to say "Gimme." But why do we suppose that God does not want us to grow up? I wouldn't respect a parent who crippled his child with a perpetual dependency. If God did that he would destroy initiative, kill ingenuity, disable us at the very point at which we are capable of being most like him, at the point of creativity. Monstrous nonsense, in the name of piety!

On this line of reasoning we could put a man on the moon with prayer, end the Middle East crisis with prayer, stop the murdering in Africa and Cambodia with prayer, and rid the human family of the scourges of disease and starvation with prayer. How about combining work and prayer? Praying won't get the lawn mowed. It may put you in the right mood to mow it, help you to be civil toward your spouse while you are mowing it, and perhaps even make you more grateful to God for grass when you have mowed it.

"I have planted, Apollos watered, but God gave the increase" (1 Cor. 3:6, KJV), wrote Paul of the growth of the church in Corinth. God did indeed give the increase, but not until Paul planted and Apollos watered. The notion that God wants us to sit back while he waits on us like a doting mama on her overweight hulk of a no-good child denies Scripture as well as intelligence. Not despite loving us, but because he loves us God wants us to struggle and work to become full-grown persons.

How does God relate to us as Father? By loving and caring for us, by guiding and disciplining us, and by rescuing us when we get in over our heads. A father who won't do all three isn't worth his salt. A father who doesn't know when which of the three is appropriate may make a perpetual emotional cripple of his child, or he may let him drown. God is a Father who will do neither.

2

A Satisfactory Friend

Some years ago a distinguished gentleman, full of years and honors, put his head down on his desk one day and unobtrusively slipped away. He died as he must have hoped to do, without bother or burden to his family, and while at work on his favorite project.

Among the multitudes of messages which came pouring in was a letter with this extraordinary observation: "He was one of the most sincere, natural, unostentatious, and completely satisfactory friends we ever had, so dependable in his homeyness and so rewarding in his kind outlook on life and all its vicissitudes."

"A completely satisfactory friend"—what a provocative description! Could one aspire to a higher calling? We use words too casually, with the result that what they stand for is sorely depreciated. "Friend" is a victim of such adulteration, but in the expression, "a completely satisfactory friend," there is the sense of something specific which is highly to be prized.

One suspects that most relationships are more nearly neighborliness and general conviviality. Thoroughly wholesome, such relationships provide a framework for the expression of sociability. They are the context for association, requiring a minimum of personal investment and maintenance. "An evening with friends," may indeed give welcome relief from the intensity of more demanding, interpersonal living.

But "a completely satisfactory friend" is not just a pleasant diversion. One wonders if in a lifetime one is able to qualify for such a name from more than a very few people. What would I be to another if I were a completely satisfactory friend? It seems to me to involve things both simple and hard.

One is that the relationship would not absorb you or lessen you as a person. This is the opposite of possessiveness which demands that the other's entire being be given up to demonstrate faithfulness to the relationship. Such an attitude is not friendship, but selfishness pure and simple. A friend does not regard another person as his "property." He does not permit himself to expect that the other is always at his beck and call.

Satisfactory friendship also allows the people involved to be comfortable in being who they are. Much of life is spent in learning carefully the art of wearing a mask to conceal feelings and views which do not meet others' approval. One can almost say that the large part of education is discovering what is unacceptable and skillfully avoiding it.

But friendship—if genuine—is a trust relationship in which the primary concern is not meeting the other's expectations but freeing the other to understand and be himself. Emerson put it eloquently: "A friend is a person with whom I may be sincere. Before him, I may think aloud. I am arrived at last in the presence of a man so real and equal, that I may drop even those undermost garments of dissimulation, courtesy, and second thought, which men never put off, and may deal with him with... simplicity and wholeness."

Akin to this is another quality—confidence in the strength of the relationship. The satisfactory friend knows and conveys a continuum of caring trust that does not require or demand constant reassurance. One sees this in the rare relationship in which two people, separated by extended periods, can meet and take up the relationship as if no separation occurred.

Emerson also had a discerning word about the sturdiness of true friendships. He said that they did not need to be treated daintily. "When they are real," he wrote, "they are not glass threads or frostwork, but the solidest thing we know."

3

Names on Our Inscription Rock

I stood beside the grave of my friend of four decades, Carlyle Marney, and remembered a lot of things he said and wrote. One was the story of Inscription Rock, a great wall in a formation called El Morro in New Mexico, guarding a pass opening to Colorado, Wyoming, Utah, and the Northwest.

In the sixteenth century the Spaniards were already using the pass. When some soldier of fortune, or later some lone trapper or prospector, came by he would cut his name, the date, and the old Spanish expression, "paso por aqui," "passed through here," into the wall. Though he might never be heard of again, that man on a given date had passed there, leaving his mark.

Everyone has his own private Inscription Rock. On it are inscribed the names and dates that tell the story of those who passed through his life and left a mark. I am sobered by my own Inscription Rock. My grandparents' names are there, etched deeply. They sheltered me and made me know that I was somebody. Miss Brown, my first teacher, wrote her name on my rock. So did some preachers of a simple gospel.

Walter Graham is there. He was the first man I ever heard who excited my mind when he preached and made me know that sermons could say something. By then I was in seminary trying to learn to preach myself.

Names of seminary teachers are there, too, for a variety of reasons. John R. Sampey, who loved Jesus Christ, King David, and Robert E. Lee, in that order but all with passion and not infrequently with tears; William Hersey Davis, who opened my eyes to the wonder of the New Testament; W. O. Carver who more than any man I had ever known made me want to learn.

Family names are all over my rock, of course. It would take a lot of space to record them, the living and the dead. An uncle saw to it that I went to college. A brother stayed home to work on the farm so I could. Inscribed are Marion and the children—the ones we have and the two we had and lost—and now the grandchildren. The list keeps growing.

Some names on my rock are there because of some unpleasantness between us. Those names and the unpleasantness seem to fade with the years, and I am glad. As shadows lengthen, the most visible names are those deeply carved by continuing relationship through joy and sorrow, thick and thin.

Moreover, on my remarkable Rock are multitudes I never met except through what they wrote—names such as Amos,

Isaiah, Job, John, and Paul. As the author of the letter to the Hebrews put it, "time would fail me to tell of" (11:32, KJV) those who put a mark on my wall with their pens. Without them I would be impoverished.

Is it not astonishing how some people seem just to happen by and leave their mark upon your life? Everyone has had the experience of being both the subject and object of encounters in which an unexpected but ineradicable impression was left.

Where is our name written above the words, "passed through here"? When people read our names on their Inscription Rocks, what do they remember and feel?

4

God's Frontier People

My grandmother was a frontier woman, pioneering twice during her long life, first as a bride in a wagon from Missouri to Texas, and then with a passel of children to the Oklahoma territory when it was opened for settlers.

When I was a child a half century ago she used to tell us exciting stories of building your own house, digging your own well, breaking the sod and planting the first crop, growing all your food, and being alone in a strange land for long periods with no neighbors for miles and your husband away building other settlers' houses.

The pioneering spirit is mankind's most important attribute. Restlessness with the known, the familiar, the established, pushes man relentlessly toward the rim of experience to search for what lies beyond. The call of the frontier is the source of all inquiry, and the fuel that powers every important achievement.

Because of it people sailed the oceans to discover new worlds, risked death to scale mountain peaks or isolate a deadly bacillus or put a man on the surface of the moon. When legitimate risks are removed, the need for risk-taking persists and people turn to phony exploits, for we are incurable frontiersmen. A safe culture is a dying one.

The longer I study the Bible the more certain I become that the essence of its message is the theme of the frontier. Abraham, our spiritual forefather, "went out, not knowing whither he went" (Heb. 11:8, KJV). The author of Hebrews expressed this impulse: "We were strangers and sojourners" (Heb. 11:13) and "Here we have no continuing city" (Heb. 13:14).

Along this line of thought Paul is our mentor. He described himself as a spiritual pilgrim, a frontiersman in search of the city of God. "I do not consider myself to have arrived, spiritually, but this one thing I do. Forgetting what lies behind, I press on toward the goal for the prize of the high calling of God in Christ Jesus" (Phil. 4:12-14). He kept hearing that "high call" every time he was tempted to give in to the temptation to settle down and take up checkers and shuffleboard.

The greatest frontier, says the Bible, is in the area of loving as God loves. It is a scary land—the land of Godlike love—full of uncertainty and risk. You may get wiped out by someone who takes advantage of your vulnerability. You will almost certainly be misunderstood, called a fool, or an unrealistic dreamer, or that worst of all epithets, a liberal.

But read the Bible and it comes down to the simple claim: "God is love, and whoever lives in love lives in God and God lives in him" (1 John 4:16).

John, who wrote those words, described life as being divided into two realms—the realm of darkness, without God, and the realm of light, with God. One is the realm of sin, hate, and death. The other is the realm of righteousness, love, and life.

Man by his unredeemed nature loves the first realm, says John, but he also hears the "clarion call," the summons of God to leave darkness and move toward the source of all light.

In the realm of darkness people operate by the rules of vengefulness, hatred, suspicion, jealousy, competitiveness, survival of the fittest, and mercilessness toward the defenseless. "Let the buyer beware" is the gospel of the kingdom of darkness.

God himself has entered this realm of death to rescue us from it, the Bible claims. He did not simply make a tourist's excursion through with the windows of his luxury car up and the doors locked. He took up residence, and became a redeeming force in the darkness. His gospel was "Love one another; as I have loved you" (John 13:34, KJV).

Ah, that is the great frontier—the frontier of living your life by the rule of love. Its limits are boundless, the possibilities as endless as God himself. How do we know that we have crossed the no-man's-land into the frontier of love? Not by professions or creeds or dogmas or pious pronouncements. We know "because we do love our brothers" (1 John 3:14). We have found a new land, a new way of regarding people, a new way of acting toward others. Here is the true frontier for every generation.

IX

Where Peace Begins

1

The Gospel's report of a song of angels announcing the Savior's birth voices mankind's deepest longing: "Glory to God in the highest, and on earth peace, good will among men" (Luke 2:14). Peace and goodwill—within and among us—there's a Christmas gift that would "go on giving."

What shall we make of the salutation to the shepherds of Bethlehem? Was it no more than a perfunctory greeting? Was it merely pious sentiment? Or was it an expression of God's will to reconcile us and heal our brokenness?

The weary world, a stench of death heavy in its nostrils, yearns for peace and goodwill among men. There is too much animosity, suspicion, and killing; there is too little peace and goodwill.

A well-nigh desperate need for personal harmony gnaws at us. We long for peace within and goodwill with those whose lives impinge upon ours. People disturbed about who and what they are come to talk of their distress. I feel their desperation and want to say, "I give you peace." But I am not God, and peace is not mine to give. Only God gives peace, and he does give it.

He invites us to believe that he gives peace, and he calls us to pray and hope for peace, both among and within ourselves. Though the prophets of old never saw its day, those men of God envisioned it. Wrote one: "It shall come to pass ... that they shall beat their swords into plowshares, and their spears into pruninghooks; nation shall not lift up sword against nation, neither shall they learn war any more" (Isa. 2:2,4, KJV). And another added to that vision: "Every man shall sit under his vine and fig tree, and none shall make them afraid" (Micah 4:4).

Such is God's purpose for the human family, not on some other planet or in heaven, but here on earth within our history. The destructive weapons are to be turned into productive tools, the energies and resources of man and nature converted into fulfillment instead of deprivation of human need, and everyone able to enjoy without fear his own place in the sun.

"Practical" people tell us condescendingly that such hopes are pious fantasies. "Never take a chance; don't stick your neck out; don't turn your back, you'll get a knife in it; others are out to get you, so get them first." Man has well-nigh impoverished the earth and exhausted himself by following such advice. Isn't it time to risk something for peace and goodwill?

Christ invites us to receive peace: "Peace I leave with you, my peace I give unto you" (John 14:27, KJV). He also calls us to be makers of peace: "Blessed are the peacemakers, for they shall be called the children of God" (Matt. 5:9, KJV).

Can we bring the vision of peace and goodwill nearer? I believe we can. We shall not do it by clinging to our fears and nursing our despair. Risk something for peace—for inner peace, for peace with your spouse or parents or children, for peace with your neighbors, for peace in the world.

We shall not do it, either, by supposing that all bad people are only good people waiting for an opportunity to do good. That is naiveté. Nor shall we bring peace closer by supposing that all virtue resides in us and all vice in others. That is arrogance. Arrogance cannot produce peace, only more arrogance and, ultimately, conflict.

Peace is strengthened every time one more person makes peace within himself by accepting the grace and love of God. If we could bring the inner hostility to an end we could focus upon reducing the tensions between ourselves and others.

Peace will be brought nearer when we are ready to declare ourselves to be brothers and sisters with all people on earth. And only then will there be hope of peace.

"Do I not destroy my enemies when I make them my friends?" Abraham Lincoln once replied to a woman's angry accusation that he wasn't destroying his enemies. Can we risk turning enemies into friends?

Gandhi once wrote of the angels' song at Bethlehem: "Today there is neither the glorifying of God nor peace on earth. As long as a hunger is not stilled and as long as we have not uprooted violence from our civilization, Christ is not yet born."

Peace and goodwill have not come everywhere. Have they come in you? Peace be in your heart. Peace be in your voice. Peace be in your eyes. Peace be in your deeds.

2

Prayer Moors Us to Solid Rock

"Lord, what a change within us one short hour/Spent in Thy presence will prevail to make!" Richard C. Trench wrote. Praying does change things. Even some who claim no relationship with God believe in praying, only they don't think it has anything to do with God. They explain it as doing hard, straight thinking and talking to yourself, sorting out the pieces of the puzzle and figuring how they go together. They describe prayer as a mustering of personal resolution and resources to overcome difficulties.

But is that all there is to prayer? If so, we had better give it another name, for such a view scarcely conceals its practical atheism. Are we merely stiffening our own backbone when we pray? Has God no interest and no hand in the outcome? Is praying merely an expression of our own best judgment, a summons by the self to the self to do the best it can? If so, then God in the biblical sense does not exist for us at all.

The soul of prayer is trust that God is such a one as Jesus called "Father." This means that he really is—not as some abstract principle, power or law—but as having identity, personhood. It means, moreover, that he is neither malevolent nor indifferent, but totally concerned about each of us as if there were only one of us to be concerned about.

Let us not pass over lightly the staggering implications of such affirmations. Man now knows better than ever his own irrelevance to time and space. If the psalmist could accept the conclusion that "we are dust" (Ps. 103:14, KJV), modern man has to deal with the realization that his entire earth is only a speck of dust suspended helplessly and temporarily in a vastness beyond man's comprehension.

Is whatever-put-it-all-together interested in my childish adulation, my half-meant pleas for deliverance from the bondage of my own wretchedness, my bewildered cries for life and peace and meaning? Yes he is, says biblical faith, but you have called him by the wrong name. He is not "whatever" but your Father.

How does God help us when we pray? Not by running to answer our summons, but by getting us to realize that he has been there all the time seeking in countless ways to get our attention so that he might help us. Read these words carefully, for they incorporate something basic about the Christian view of prayer: "I sought the Lord, and afterward I knew he moved my heart to it who sought for me."

St. Augustine put it in a simple parable. He said that when a man in a boat throws a rope to a rock, it is not to pull the rock to the boat, but the boat to the rock. Prayer, then, is mooring our boat to the solid rock.

But it is more. Prayer will not change God's will, but it will put us where he can do his will through us. Prayer cannot divert the stream of life, but it can put our lives into the stream. Emerson once said that the Gulf Stream "will flow through a wheat straw if it is laid parallel to the current." Prayer is laying your life, its resources and its possibilities parallel to the will of God.

In all of this you will note that nothing has been said about God sparing the prayer from hardship, sorrow, and failure. That is not an oversight. The Bible makes no such promise. It does promise that through prayer we can cope with life. Learning to cope with it, learning to handle it, to manage it—ah, that is the victory! And here we have confidence that prayer changes things.

One other thing must be added. Prayer is not a substitute for, but an addition to the exercise of our best self. The person morally sick is not apt to get well by simply making up his mind to do so, but neither will he overcome his problem by accusing God of failing to help him when he won't do anything to help himself.

3

The Patience of Unanswered Prayer

"Teach me the patience of unanswered prayer," reads a line from a familiar hymn ("Spirit of God, Descend Upon My Heart"), reflecting common human experience with God. Sometimes we don't feel he is nigh, and we do struggle, doubt, rebel, and sense no answer to our prayers. People who claim never to have had these feelings must be more spiritual than Jesus. He confessed to them. His prayer in Gethsemane and his cry from the cross encourage us ordinary believers.

Jesus spoke frequently about prayer, which should surprise no one, for what is more important than communion with God our Father? However, he had no use for pretentious, long-winded praying. Jesus continually encouraged his disciples to pray boldly and intimately. "Ask, ... seek, ... knock" (Matt. 7:7, KJV), he said. Don't be timid about approaching God with your needs. "If you then, who are evil, know how to give good gifts to your children, how much more will your Father who is in heaven give good things to those who ask him!" (Matt. 7:11, RSV). On the scale of one to infinity the parent's love for the child, the best we know, is infinitely less than the heavenly Father's love. If a good parent does not ignore his child, let us be assured that God will not turn his back upon us.

Luke's Gospel records a parable Jesus told to encourage his followers "always to pray and not lose heart" (Luke 18:1, RSV). There is no question but that Jesus believed the limitation to prayer's effectiveness is mainly imposed by ourselves.

Is it not presumptuous to decide what God can and cannot do, or what he should or should not do? Who are we to regulate God? "Ask," Jesus said. Give God an opportunity to help.

In the beautiful story in Genesis of Isaac's birth to Abraham and Sarah in their childless old age, God announced the forthcoming event and said to their wondering questions: "Is anything too hard for the Lord?" (Gen. 18:14). It is an appropriate challenge to those who claim to believe in him. However, the experience which prompted the line in the hymn verse is relevant: "Teach me the patience of unanswered prayer." Is prayer ever unanswered? Perhaps not. No is an answer, though not the one we like to hear.

Prayers that ask God to do what is contrary to his nature are unanswered. How can I ask him to violate his God-ness just to please me? During World War II a magazine story entitled "Twelve-Thirty P.M." was about a scheme to assassinate Hitler by prayer. In this piece of fiction a Midwest farmer proposed a worldwide meeting to get rid of Hitler through simultaneous, concentrated praying.

But prayer is not a magic device to control other people, to overcome their evil intentions. Whatever God does, he has made it plain that he will not take away our freedom to do with our lives what we are determined to do, even if it means our destruction. Jesus must have prayed for Judas daily, but Judas betrayed him nonetheless. Prayer is not a means for gaining advantage over others. "Help me run faster, hit harder, outwit the opposition," does not strike me as the kind of prayer God will honor and grant.

The bottom line is that while on the one hand we are continually encouraged to pray without ceasing, on the other hand the testimony of Scripture confirms our own experience that we do not always receive what we ask. Paul prayed fervently to be relieved of his thorn in the flesh but was told, "My grace is sufficient for you to bear this affliction and convert it into a means of blessing for others" (2 Cor. 12:9). Was Paul's prayer answered? Yes, but it was an answer he had rather not have heard. Only afterward, as he saw how that thorn had been transformed into a blessing, could he have understood why God wouldn't remove it.

X

Who Says You're Through?

1

When All Speak Well of You

A disturbing statement appears in Luke's version of our Lord's Sermon on the Mount: "Woe to you, when all men speak well of you" (6:26, RSV). That is a hard saying, for it contradicts the aim and cherished hopes of most of us. Everybody wants to make all the friends and influence all the people he can. We want men to speak well of us.

More than that, the saying contradicts the way most of us were brought up. "A good name is rather to be chosen than great riches" (Prov. 22:1, KJV), was an oft-quoted Scripture verse in our home. To gain the respect and good opinion of others was taught as an important endeavor. So deeply ingrained is this desire that we look askance at anyone who flaunts public opinion.

Not only is it normal to want approval of others, it even seems necessary to healthy existence. Movie stars can see their careers ascend on the stairway of scandal, but most of us would be ruined by it. The man in public office, the minister in the pulpit, the merchant in business, the teacher in the class-

Who Says You're Through? / 153

room, all are dependent upon public approval. What one's public image is can never be separated from one's effectiveness in his work. So important is reputation that even the law protects one from being falsely accused. Some of the most celebrated law cases of the past decade have concerned attacks upon people's good names.

This is why gossip is such a vicious and dastardly sin. We often intend no real harm when we gossip, but we may unintentionally injure someone more seriously than if we did bodily harm.

Some are even concerned about what people will think of them after they are dead. That is one of the strongest motivations for charitable works.

Now, with this strong need for approval, what are we to do with Jesus' flat statement: "Woe to you, when all men speak well of you"?

To put it simply, these words mean that if we are pleasing everybody we had better watch out, for we can't be pleasing God. Unless you are like the chameleon, adjusting your color to suit whatever background surrounds you, it is impossible to have all men speak well of you. The moment you are hearing all praise and getting no abuse, you ought to start worrying and ask yourself, "Am I so compromising my principles that I stand for nothing?"

To want all men to speak well of you is a dangerous desire. It may make a coward of you when you ought to speak or act. It may feed your insecurity, leaving you destitute every time the goddess of fortune frowns, or unduly inflating your ego when some inconsequential plum is dropped in your lap.

That person who stands for something will inevitably be criticized. This is true for two simple reasons. First, we do not like those who are different; it is a threat to us because it suggests we might be wrong. Second, standing for something often distinguishes between superiority and mediocrity. Mediocrity cannot endure excellence. He who puts his head above the crowd is going to have potshots taken at him.

The only security a man can find is in being primarily concerned with doing right as he sees it, being thus equally impervious to praise or blame. It is no good to listen to the sweet strains of flattery and compliment and then close one's ears to discordant notes of criticism.

It is only when we are strong enough to receive praise without being spoiled that we shall become brave enough to accept blame and criticism without being undone. The man who puts his back in a position to be patted is also exposing it to be kicked.

Samuel Johnson understood this, and in one of his prayers he asked to be made strong enough that neither praise would fill him with pride nor censure with discontent.

2

Genuine Thankfulness

It is not easy for modern Americans, impressed with their own competence and preoccupied with today's problems, to feel or express gratitude. And more's the pity, for life is incomplete in the measure that appreciation is missing. Further, it is the ingredient whose absence turns the recipe into a sour, unpleasant mess.

You will know examples of the mess—the nasty slob who lies on his back and invents new words to curse the world because it has not given him more, or the arrogant snob who is just as certain that he owes nobody anything. Between these extremes are most of us, trying to live our lives with a measure of openness, a healthy appreciation for our heritage, and a wholesome commitment to life and to the God who put us here. This is authentic gratitude.

It arises out of the awareness that one is indebted. "I am debtor," wrote Paul, "to all men" (Rom. 1:14). We all are, but admitting it is not easy. It requires owning up to our incompleteness and inadequacy. It is flattering to be needed; it is hard to need. To be needed makes one master; to need makes one supplicant. To have something to give brings the exhilaration of power; to have to be given something may bring resentment and depression.

Gratitude is the grace to accept dependency without becoming dependent or resentful. With gratitude, one can acknowledge life's "givenness" without losing dignity. Perhaps that is why the Bible sings with continual praise of God, thanksgiving flowing from its pages in a continual stream. Perhaps that explains the irresistible charm of New Testament faith. Its constant note was, "Thanks be to God for his inexpressible gift!" (2 Cor. 9:15, RSV).

Material abundance has only the most casual relationship to genuine thankfulness. It may even make gratitude come harder. If we have never known what it is to be hungry, how can we be grateful for being full? If we have never been cold, how can we fully appreciate warmth? If we have never known sorrow, how can we know joy?

As gratitude's source is not in having, neither is it in comparative well-being. We ought not to base our gratitude on the fact that we don't have somebody else's problems. That poor reason for being thankful nearly always leads to self-congratulation, like the Pharisee of Jesus' parable: "I thank thee, Lord, that I am not as other men are" (Luke 18:11).

Can I congratulate myself for being well on the basis that so many others are sick? Can I be thankful that I have plenty when millions live and die in want? Shall I respond to my awareness of others' need by thanking God that I am not in need? Shall the spirit of gratitude in me rise on the winds of my brother's adversity?

In the disturbing play, *The Deputy,* a young priest is protesting the inaction of his church when Italian Jews are being deported by the trainload to concentration camps and gas chambers. In a frenzy of emotion he cries, "Are we to stand by and wave our handkerchiefs to them. . . . And then—then we go home. . . . And sit down to some journal, to read about the excavations in St. Peter's?"

Gratitude lies in the realization that life is a gift. When man views himself and his condition as the basis of deciding whether or not to be grateful, he is always left the choices of self-pity or self-commendation. Only when God becomes his focus, only in acceptance of the life he has given us to live, is gratitude possible.

3

The Right Kind of Patriotism

A lot of people in this country are both patriotic and religious but leery of "patriotism" and "religion." What turns them off is saying what we don't mean, like "one Nation under God, indivisible, with liberty and justice for all." To be sure, there is an inescapable gap between our ideals and our achievements. Thank God our professions are better than our practices.

Nevertheless, it is not good enough to let the word stand for the deed. The vast majority of young people are passionately devoted to the goals of the American democratic dream, impatient to see it implemented. They are concerned about the quality of life they and their children are going to have. Why does that enrage so many of us who are their elders? Would we rather they didn't care?

Moreover, contrary to the bilge spewed out by some of their self-appointed saviors, the youth are learning that they can participate in the shaping of the future. They can have a piece of the action. When a man makes that discovery he picks up new enthusiasm. He has a reason to get involved.

So we are going to see many young people engaged in the political arena, seeking to make an impact through the public forum and the ballot. Let us salute their courage and idealism, while reminding them and ourselves that the workability of the democratic process depends upon persuasion and participation.

It is the slow, long way around to getting the right thing done. But it beats anything yet imagined for man's governing of himself. To seek to get wrong righted through persuasion and by the use of law is our best hope.

A lot is wrong, and when this rising generation gives way to its successor there still will be. New situations always bring new problems. They always outrun man's ability to cope with them. We are still wrestling with the problems of the industrial revolution—technology, mass production, waste, leisure, the city; to say nothing of social, economic, and moral problems emerging from the space age!

We should encourage political activity by all citizens because it is one of the ways by which a man expresses his responsibility to God. Citizenship is not only a civil but a religious obligation. A man's first obligation is to God as God has come to him through his religious heritage. There is no question about that.

"Thou shalt love the Lord thy God" (Deut. 6:5, KJV) and "Thou shalt have none other gods before me" (Deut. 5:7, KJV) are absolute requirements.

How does man validate his obligation to serve God? In the living of his life—every act, relationship, response becomes an expression of either fidelity or infidelity to God. He does what he does either as an obedient or as a disobedient child of God.

Unlike Jews or Christians living in the Roman Empire in the first century AD, you and I live under a government which we ourselves have helped to make. We are a part of it. Some of us may even be among those elected by our peers. So each of us has a responsibility for it. We have lawful means of redress when we believe that it is treating us or others unjustly. We can change it by persuading others at election that a different leadership in government is needed.

I write as an American, for that is what I am. No sense can be made of my relationships with the world, no matter how universal my viewpoint, except from the realization that I am an American. The traditions of this nation are mine and yours. And they also belong to the young. Neither they nor we should forget it.

Nearly seventy years ago, on the occasion of the coronation of King George V of England, a young minister who was to become archbishop of Canterbury and one of twentieth-century Christendom's greatest figures, William Temple, preached. "If we are to be good men, it must be by becoming good Englishmen; there is no other way open to us," he said. "We are born members of a nation whose character has been given a very definite form by its peculiar history."

That is the kind of patriotism which needs espousing to this generation. It neither apologizes nor shouts with arrogance that all others are inferior. It gratefully acknowledges its own heritage and hopefully resolves to pass on to its inheritors the dream more fully realized.

4

Work: Blessing or Curse?

There is more to life than showing up for work every time the bell rings, but work is an integral, indispensable part of a full life. To want to do something with one's life, to aspire to usefulness, is the mark of a fine human being. What we require of our occupation, then, is a sense of meaning, a sense of achievement, however modest.

Popular wisdom holds that happiness would be living on a balmy island where the most arduous labor of the day would be reaching up to pick a piece of fruit. In such a place it isn't likely man would develop much of a civilization. But a lot of us act as if work is a burden, an unpleasantness to be avoided, a necessity to be endured. That is an evil and tragically harmful attitude.

The person who finds no satisfaction and takes no pride in his work has deprived himself of one of life's rewarding experiences. Most of us will spend forty hours a week fifty weeks a year for forty-five years working. Just to go through the motions, merely earning money so that we can "live" during the remaining hours, is a waste of 90,000 hours out of a man's life.

We can be thankful, of course, that we no longer live in sweatshop days with sunup to sundown hours of backbreaking labor. But schedules, timetables, and clocks all have their place. We need the discipline they provide. He who eats the bread of idleness as a continual diet soon gets indigestion of the spirit.

Yes, work is good. It provides life's necessities, affects favorably our self-esteem, keeps us constructively and happily busy, helps us to express what we are, and enables us to find meaning in something which will outlast us.

But work also can be a curse. History shows that work more often has been a burden rather than a blessing. This truth is recognized in the Genesis account of man's creation and fall. Man was never a freeloading visitor in the garden; he had a job to do—farming and tending the place. But man's sin affected not only his relationship with God and his fellowman but also with the natural order. God told man that his sin "cursed ... the ground" (Gen. 3:17, KJV) and made it an enemy of man's efforts to work it. Note that God did not curse man to work. Work itself was not a punishment, but man's sin set man against nature and nature against man.

Work remains honorable, even for God. Jesus spoke of his Father as "working still" (John 5:17a, RSV). God has not retired. He is not sitting on his throne whittling a stick. "And I work" (John 5:17, KJV), Jesus said. The apostle Paul believed in work. He supported himself by making tents. It is plain in his letters that he had no use for lazy, trifling people. There is no question about the Bible's view of work, but work is not everything, and we need to discard some strange notions about it.

One such notion is that a person's worth is determined by the kind of work he does. We attach too much significance to a person's vocation; it largely determines the respect and admiration we have for others. A college president proved it true. During summer he worked as a garbage collector. When he asked for a drink of water at back doors, he was often turned away. That same man, had he been recognized, would have been welcomed into the parlor.

Another bad notion about work is that there is the right job for you if you could just find it. Looking for the "right" place prevents our settling down to make creative use of the place we have. All life is flawed, and if we found a perfect job, we would be unsuited for it because we ourselves are not perfect.

Another faulty view is that work is only a necessary evil, a means to afford a higher standard of living, but a shame to have to earn it that way. But work never dehumanized anyone unless he let it. I am not made a slave to my job unless I have a slave mentality. I prefer to think of myself as a free person who has chosen to work to meet the needs of myself and others with whom I am interdependent. Many needs of mine require the work of other people. Our lives are lived in the honorable fashion of exchanging goods and services.

While it is true that work is a way of paying your own way, there are times when we can't do it and must call on our brothers and sisters for help. It is not ignoble to need help. We are dehumanized only if we are too trifling to work or if society has made it impossible for us to earn our way.

Whether work is a blessing or a curse is determined more by our attitudes than by our occupation. We need to recognize that because God created us in his image, he made us also to create. To realize that one's work is at least a potential partnership with God would revolutionize many an office or plant. Life would take on meaning that higher pay and shorter hours can never give.

5

The Tyranny of Wealth

The commands of Jesus appear to be so disarmingly simple that we are apt to pay scant heed. Perhaps familiarity has bred contempt. Maybe we have heard his stirring calls and done nothing about them so often that our decision-making apparatus has been short-circuited. It would be a great day for Christianity if people could again feel the exciting, awesome impact of what Paul once termed "the high calling of God in Christ Jesus" (Phil. 3:14, KJV).

Take as example one of the most familiar of all our Lord's sayings: "Seek ye first the kingdom of God, and his righteousness, and all these things shall be added unto you" (Matt. 7:33, KJV). Now what can this mean to a twentieth-century person? What if God really did reign in our individual and corporate life?

For one thing, these words are a stern warning against the tyranny of things. Material things do tyrannize us. They make slaves out of us so that many a wife becomes a slave to a beautiful house and many a man becomes a slave to his job or estate. It is next to impossible for a child to grow up in our midst without being infected with the admiring, adoring, almost worshiping preoccupation with the material goods and physical pleasures of life.

The warning was first spoken to simple Galilean peasants who had "left all and followed" (Mark 10:28) Jesus. They probably had no more than two shirts to their backs. Yet he warned them against the tyranny of things, for he knew that the love of material possessions and physical pleasures is a grave temptation to any human being. If he saw it as a temptation to the people of his day, what would he say to our secularized, goods-centered generation?

I point this out, not because I think we would be better off if our vast storehouse of technological conveniences were suddenly taken away, but because I think we are extremely vulnerable.

We are endangered because life naturally moves from the simple to the complex. Few people start out to bury themselves under a pile of hardware or real estate. We just want enough to be comfortable. But few of us are wise enough to know when that point has been reached. As one of our economic tycoons said in the early twentieth century when asked how much money is enough, "Always just a little bit more than you've got!" We rarely ever have grit or religion enough to reverse the process toward increasing thing-centeredness unless disaster or misfortune compels us.

Another danger of money and things which money can buy is that we become proud and self-sufficient. Our hearts have been stolen away, and we have ceased to think of life as an entrustment and our material blessings as gifts. It is exceedingly difficult for a person who has only to reach for his checkbook to get whatever his heart desires to feel that he actually owes life very much.

Success had been the undoing of multitudes who might have endured hardship with no diminution of character. It is more than a proverb that some people cannot stand prosperity.

But it may be that the worst enslavement of wealth is not what it does to those who possess it, but what it makes them do to other people. Money affects our vision, blinding us to the needs and the worth of others. Jesus said it like this: "If thine eye be sound, then thy whole body is full of light. If thine eye be faulty, then thy whole body be full of darkness" (Matt. 6:22-23).

If we were to put this in modern parlance we would say, If you have got the almighty dollar so close to your eye that it shuts out the vision of everything else, then you cannot see what is going on around you.

This is why Jesus warned so sternly against getting too attached to things. "You cannot love God and wealth" (Matt. 6:24), he declared.

6

Who Says You're Through?

I know an eighty-year-old man who is still teaching in a technical school. This sprightly octogenarian first retired at seventy-one, came out of retirement to take a college teaching job three years later, retired again, and now is back in harness.

Granted, he is unusual. But Carl Sandburg was still writing poetry at eighty-five, Grandma Moses painting at 101. Frank Lloyd Wright designed the Guggenheim Museum at seventy-six, and Winston Churchill was reelected British prime minister at seventy-seven. Dr. Albert Schweitzer won the Nobel Peace Prize at sixty-eight and thereafter continued his unselfish labors as missionary doctor in Lambarene, Gabon, until his death at ninety.

We aren't all Sandburgs or Schweitzers. We lack their intelligence, energy, and arteries. One suspects, however, that a great many of us also lack their spirit and will. Now that science is keeping us alive so much longer, it seems sensible to think about how to make more of the extra years.

Someone put it graphically: We are in the position of a man who suddenly finds that his day lasts forty-eight hours instead of twenty-four. How will he use time to take account of his new situation? Well, he can't wait until they hand him his first Social Security check to begin thinking about it. The tragedy of old age is having refused to think beyond middle age and its productivity.

One's faculties start to decline at twenty, but one's mental capacity grows to its full development only around thirty-five, and maintains a high level to the most advanced age. Unfortunately, most of us stop learning and give up any effort to achieve greater mental and emotional maturity by the time we hit thirty-five, just when our mental capacities are reaching their potential.

If you are getting older—and if you are alive you are—stop thinking of yourself as a piece of machinery that is steadily being worn-out and will eventually be moved to the junkyard. Your company may have mandatory retirement at sixty-five, but retirement from the place where you presently earn your paycheck need not mean retirement from useful life.

Keep up physical and mental activity without intermission. Nothing is more disintegrating than stagnation and resignation. Who knows how many people die—mentally, emotionally, and even physically—just because they simply "roll over and give up"? A physician, writing about old age, described it as a state in which one does more and more things for the last time and fewer and fewer things for the first time. His suggestion for avoiding drying up in old age is to reverse the process: continue to do as many things as possible for the first time and try to give up as little as possible.

Remain open to new ideas, and fresh information about old ideas. How long has it been since you really changed your mind about anything that matters? Do you like younger people, or are you afraid they will be too "radical" for you to be comfortable? Do you fear being around them because you are afraid they will not respect your age? When you talk to young people, do you listen to what they are saying, or do you insist on lecturing them about "the good old days"? These questions inquire into your flexibility, an important index to whether you are growing old gracefully.

Take a careful look at your attitude toward change. That is a significant barometer of your emotional aging process. Have you been anywhere new, made any new friends, done anything nice for somebody else, written a letter of appreciation or protest, read a mind-stretching book, seen a provocative movie, talked to someone interesting about something other than the condition of your intestines or the state of your arthritis?

Watch out for the temptation to take yourself too seriously. Perhaps you have done well in life. Maybe you are even important. But never permit yourself the suspicion that you are indispensable. Set the world down, Atlas, you don't need to carry it on your back. It will get along surprisingly well without you. So relax and think about who you are, what is happening to you, and how you can give more to life while you are here.

However old you are—or young—you are not through until you give up. There is no way to remove the uncertainty, take away all the aches and pains, undo some of the mistakes, wipe out some of the regrets, get over some of the griefs. But life need never be dull, and sometimes it can be surpassingly beautiful to the very end.